AF261830

BLUEPRINT OF A KILLER

Monsters in the Making, from Childhood to Murder

HEATHER MROCZENSKI, M.S., BCBA, LBA

WildBluePress.com

Blueprint of a Killer published by:
WILDBLUE PRESS
P.O. Box 102440
Denver, Colorado 80250

Publisher Disclaimer: Any opinions, statements of fact or fiction, descriptions, dialogue, and citations found in this book were provided by the author, and are solely those of the author. The publisher makes no claim as to their veracity or accuracy, and assumes no liability for the content.

Copyright 2026 by Heather Mroczenski

All rights reserved. No part of this book may be reproduced in any form or by any means without the prior written consent of the Publisher, excepting brief quotes used in reviews.

WILDBLUE PRESS is registered at the U.S. Patent and Trademark Offices.

ISBN 978-1-970361-14-8 Hardcover
ISBN 978-1-970361-15-5 Trade Paperback
ISBN 978-1-970361-13-1 eBook

Cover design © 2026 WildBlue Press. All rights reserved.

Interior Formatting and Book Cover Design by Elijah Toten
www.totencreative.com

BLUEPRINT OF A KILLER

CONTENTS

NOTE FROM THE AUTHOR

Like every basic white girl, I've been fascinated with serial killers and crime for as long as I can remember. Naturally, I looked up how to be in the FBI and may have even emailed the FBI at least once to see if it was a career I could pursue. I've listened to all the true crime podcasts, seen all the shows, and watched *Criminal Minds* at least two times through. I've always been captivated not by the crimes themselves, but by the people behind the crimes; the individuals who, for whatever reason, became killers.

Instead of analyzing crime as a career, I've kept it as a hobby and chosen behavior analysis as a career… somewhat similar, but also… not. I work as a Board-Certified Behavior Analyst (BCBA), which means I study and shape behavior. Most of the time, that looks like working with autistic kids, helping them learn new skills, managing behaviors that interfere with learning, and ultimately improving their independence and quality of life. ABA, which stands for Applied Behavior Analysis, is a science, a systematic way of understanding how behavior works and using that knowledge to help people learn what they want to learn and reduce behaviors that get in the way. It's the reason I know, for example, how to teach a child to communicate their needs instead of melting down or how to help a student go from refusing to do a task to completing it successfully.

ABA isn't just for autistic kids, though. It can be used successfully for anyone, whether it be an autistic child with behavioral difficulties, a husband who still can't seem to remember to put the toilet seat down, or a dog who refuses to eat the food you've bought for her. It's about learning what motivates behavior, what maintains it, and how to teach and reinforce new behaviors. Understanding behavior in this structured way is also why ABA can be useful for learning about criminals. While murder is never something that should be excused, you can start to see the patterns, the reinforcements, and the environment that shaped them. You can start to see the blueprint of a killer.

My love for learning about serial killers has never been about the crimes themselves but about what made the criminal in the first place. Why are they the way that they are? What experiences did they go through? Were they born this way, or was it their environment? Murder is unforgivable, but what makes the murderer? What is it in their past, in their relationships, in their brain, and in the circumstances around them that creates a person capable of such actions? I want to understand the blueprint because, in my mind, understanding it means you understand a little more about the why behind the unthinkable.

I decided to write this book on a whim because I was looking for a book exactly like this and couldn't find one, but it also seems like something that's been building for my entire life, driven by my fascination with psychology and understanding people.

I listened to a podcast once called *Imagined Life* by Wondery, where they told the entire story of a famous person's life without revealing who it was until the very end. I loved it. I loved the thrill of guessing who the story was about, and I loved focusing on the story itself, not just the celebrity. That's exactly what I wanted for this book: for the reader to focus on what shaped the killers' lives rather than on the killers themselves. The whys matter more than the horror, and the formative experiences matter more than the headlines.

I also wanted to approach this in a way that made the science of behavior approachable. ABA taught me to break things down into pieces, to look at antecedents and consequences, to ask what motivates behavior, and to look for patterns across time. That same thinking applies to understanding serial killers. Every small act, every trauma, every reinforcement and punishment, every exposure to violence or neglect; all of it contributes to building a blueprint. When you study a killer's life from this perspective, it's not about sensationalizing the acts but about understanding the trajectory.

Working in ABA has also helped me notice the subtleties in behavior that others might miss. I see how early exposure to reinforcement or punishment shapes responses, how modeling behavior affects learning, and how some behaviors become "fixed" or habitual without conscious awareness. These same principles, in a darker sense, can be applied to criminals. You can look at the way someone's early environment, traumas, and opportunities reinforced certain impulses. You can see how small behaviors snowballed into dangerous patterns. You can look for the blueprint.

I hope readers will come away with more than just a sense of the crimes, but with an understanding of human patterns, reinforcement history, environmental shaping, and personal traumas that contributed to each person's blueprint. I hope they will understand that curiosity about why doesn't equal sympathy for the actions, and that knowledge of the blueprint isn't about absolution but about comprehension. Most of all, I hope they will enjoy the thrill of trying to guess what shaped the person, as I did with Imagined Life, and in doing so, focus less on the killers themselves and more on how they came to be.

PROLOGUE

Born to a drug-addicted mother and put into abusive foster home after abusive foster home, he was five when he accidentally discovered the power and control he gained from feeling the life drain out of small, helpless animals. It started with the family rabbit that "died in her sleep" and progressed to the teacup Pomeranian who "tripped over a toy." Alone in a house of adults who wanted nothing to do with him until they were drunk or angry, he learned early that he couldn't control what happened to him, but he could control what he did to others.

You've heard it before - life is made up of small moments. From the first breath out of our mothers' womb, our brain is deciding what kind of person we'll one day become. Most of us have fairly insignificant childhoods with perhaps some mild "trauma" that may at most provide our future therapists with years of interesting stories to tell at cocktail parties. For some, though, the capital T Trauma experienced at a young age causes an impact that will be dissected by behavior analysts, FBI agents, child psychologists, and couch detectives for decades to come.

Research[1] consistently shows a strong connection between childhood abuse and later serial killer behavior. Early abuse may desensitize individuals to pain and violence and contribute to distorted cognitive processing, such as hostile attribution biases and aggressive thought patterns. Studies also reveal that individuals who kill for sexual gratification are significantly more likely to have experienced various forms of abuse, particularly psychological and physical, compared to non-offenders. Roughly half of serial killers report psychological abuse, over a third report physical abuse, and one-quarter report sexual abuse.

Dr. Bruce Perry's *The Boy Who Was Raised as a Dog* vividly illustrates how early childhood experiences shape brain development, emotional regulation, and later behavior. Through real clinical cases, Perry demonstrates that trauma in early life doesn't just affect emotions; it literally alters brain structure and function. Children who endure neglect, abuse, or chronic fear develop maladaptive patterns for processing stress, attachment, and empathy, which can persist into adulthood if not properly addressed. His work underscores the idea that early trauma doesn't excuse violent behavior. Still, it helps explain how disrupted attachment, lack of safety, and repeated exposure to fear can distort normal developmental pathways. Perry's findings provide a crucial psychological foundation for understanding how many serial killers' early environments may have shaped their capacity for empathy, impulse control, and moral reasoning.[3]

From an applied behavior analysis perspective, what a child experiences shapes who they become in very concrete ways. Every interaction, every caregiver response, and every moment of fear or comfort teach the brain what works, what is safe, and what is dangerous. In homes filled with neglect or abuse, behaviors like aggression, cruelty to animals, or extreme withdrawal aren't random; they're learned strategies, reinforced by the child's environment. Behavior analysis helps us see these patterns not as excuses, but as clues to how early life molds behavior over time.

When it comes to early childhood development, one of the central experiences is touch. Human development begins with physical connection. Touch is one of the first ways an infant experiences the world and forms a sense of safety and attachment. Before birth, the developing child exists in an environment of constant containment and movement. After birth, that expectation of closeness continues through being held, carried, and physically comforted by caregivers. These early experiences play a significant role in shaping the brain and nervous system across mammalian species. What remains less understood is how disruptions in early physical connection may influence higher-level outcomes later in life, including social behavior, emotional regulation, and moral development.[2]

Physical touch in early childhood is such a simple thing, but a make-or-break experience for healthy development. When loving caregivers feed, hug, and respond to their infant's needs with warmth and consistency, the child's brain, nervous system, and capacity for trust and emotional regulation are strengthened. When caregivers use touch to abuse an infant physically or sexually, or when touch is absent due to neglect, it disrupts the development of stress regulation, attachment, and social-emotional functioning, leaving lasting vulnerabilities that can affect behavior well into adulthood.

These patterns of early trauma are not just theoretical; they can be seen in the childhoods of some of history's most notorious serial killers. Take Edmund Kemper, for example. He grew up in a dysfunctional household and from the very young age of five was reportedly verbally abused and emotionally isolated. His mother frequently humiliated him and treated him with hostility, creating an environment of fear and low self-worth. He grew up to murder his grandparents and later multiple young women, displaying extreme violence and psychological detachment. Many would say he never stood a chance. Or what about Albert Fish? He grew up in a household marked by neglect and early sexual abuse, and from a very young age, he was exposed to sadistic practices and beatings. His caregivers failed to provide safety or affection, and he grew up to commit gruesome acts of murder and cannibalism. Peter Sutcliffe, the "Yorkshire Ripper," grew up in a controlling and emotionally distant household, experiencing frequent humiliation and emotional neglect from his parents. He later became a serial killer who targeted women mostly in northern England, showing how early deprivation and punitive parenting may have fueled rage and misogyny.

Not all childhood trauma leads to a future of psychopathy and serial killing. Many children who experience neglect or abuse go on to live healthy, productive lives, highlighting the complex interplay of resilience, environment, and individual temperament. The goal of this book is not to suggest inevitability, but to narrow in on the early lives of ten serial killers to explore how their childhood experiences shaped who they became and the patterns that emerged in their adult behavior.

What we will experience together in the coming chapters are stories of ten serial killers and the lives they went on to live. But more importantly, we'll see the importance of early childhood experience and intervention. You, as a reader, will start each story blindfolded, with no knowledge of whose childhood you are reading about. Piece by piece, you'll see how formative experiences, small choices, and moments of neglect or care are combined to shape the person they became. These stories are not meant to evoke empathy (although they likely will) but rather an understanding of the circumstances that can and have historically come together in the making of a serial killer.

PART 1

YOU SHOULD BE MINE

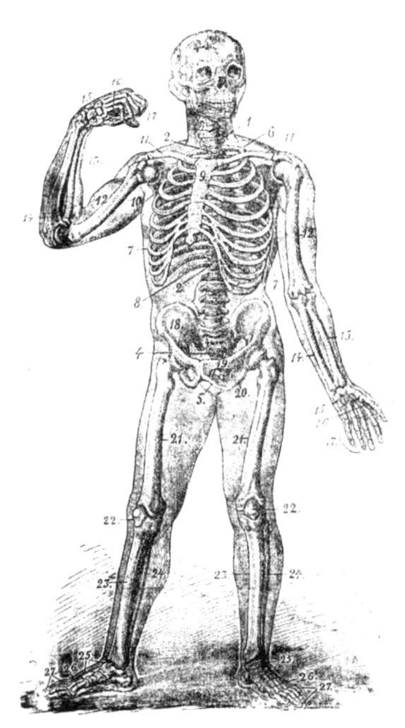

CHAPTER 1

On a cool Midwestern morning in 1964, a quaint house stands silently overlooking its surroundings against the backdrop of trees. Inside, the smell of cheap but potent whiskey lingers in the air, mixing with the sound of cursing and shattering ceramic. A blonde-haired boy with thick, black glasses sits at the kitchen table, tracing lines with his finger into the wood. His face is blank, his stare emotionless. He ignores the chaos surrounding him, just as he is so often ignored.

When we zoom into this child's life, it's not hard to see where it all went wrong. To understand how a boy in that kitchen became one of America's most infamous killers, we must start at the beginning - before the headlines, before the horror, and inside the early environment that shaped him.

It was 1959 in Wisconsin when, after two months of marriage, the boy's parents discovered they were expecting. But what began as a quick, hopeful beginning soon unraveled into a difficult pregnancy filled with illness, stress, and growing strain between them. Having experienced severe nausea, anxiety, muscle stiffness, and other health issues, the boy's mother was on a concoction of 26 pills per day. Her illness forced her to quit her job and stay home, but her problems only increased from there. She became increasingly nervous and bothered by seemingly small things, such as the noises and odors from her downstairs neighbors, and irritated by her husband's lack of concern about the same things. It got to the point where they had no choice but to move in with his parents, with whom neither of them had a good relationship. She also began experiencing an undiagnosed seizure-like rigidity where her legs and body would lock into place, grow rigid, and then begin to tremble. For this, the doctors added another medication to her growing list of drugs. The boy's father did what he could to keep his wife comfortable. Still, as a graduate student studying analytical chemistry, he was gone most of the day, often leaving at 7 am and not returning until 7 or 8 pm. Without a driver's license and essentially housebound with in-laws she didn't get along with, it's no wonder the boy's mother felt anxious and irritated much of the time.[5]

After 9 long months, on May 21, 1960, our story's villain was born.

When he came home from the hospital, the boy had one of his small legs wrapped in a cast that was meant to fix a minor deformity, but he was otherwise healthy. The two parents were living in bliss as a new family of 3. Unfortunately, though, that bliss ended quickly. The boy's mother had trouble nursing for a reason she couldn't name and began to dread it, quickly giving it up completely. The boy shared a room with his parents in his grandparents' house, so space was tight, and there was no short supply of tension and arguments. His mother grew increasingly irritated at her mother-in-law, and it wasn't long before she sequestered herself in the upstairs room. Feeling helpless and confused, the boy's father began avoiding his wife and home as much as possible, throwing himself into work and school. This worked until it didn't. Four months into the boy's life, the family moved out of the grandparents' house and into a one-bedroom apartment.[5]

The next several years of the boy's life were relatively average. He was happy, talkative, and always giggling about something. He played with toys, built blocks, and ripped up leaves just like any other little boy his age. When he was about 2 years old, life continued in Iowa, where the boy's father got a new job. The new house was smaller and older than the first apartment, causing extreme anxiety in the boy's mother as she attempted to keep the house free of clutter and turn it into a home. Even in these seemingly ordinary years, the undercurrent of conflict and instability was never far from the surface.[5]

The cycle of irritation from the mother and avoidance from the father continued as their relationship deteriorated. Fights worsened and would often become physical, with the boy's mom grabbing kitchen knives and threatening to stab her husband on multiple occasions. On top of their marital problems, they had a child who was constantly suffering through one illness or another. Whether it was an ear infection or a bug that severely disturbed his throat, the boy was in and out of the university clinic as they dealt with his ailments.[5]

One day in 1964, the boy started complaining of a tenderness in his groin area. This tenderness worsened and a new bulge appeared on his scrotum. After taking him to the doctor, his parents learned that the boy was suffering from a double hernia that was the result of a birth defect, and that the only course of action was surgery. The surgery was successfully performed one week later, and he returned home a few days after that. The doctor reported that the surgery went well; however, he was in a lot of pain immediately after and asked his mother if the doctors had cut off his penis.

Recovery was hard. The boy spent long hours in a bathrobe laying on his sofa, moving slowly, seemingly drained of all energy. His personality flattened, and family members remarked that his demeanor seemed to shift permanently from bubbly and thriving to more withdrawn, less energetic, and emotionally detached. While there are no direct ties between the surgery and this shift in mood, research shows a statistically significant link between undergoing hernia repair before the age of three (the boy was four) and a higher likelihood of developing behavioral or developmental disorders.[2] There are also findings that suggest that more frequent exposure to surgery and anesthesia, especially at a younger age or lower body weight, may have adverse effects on cognitive and behavioral development.[3]

Over the next two years the boy continued to grow more inward, often sitting quietly and motionless for long periods of time with no expression on his face. Looking back at pictures of that time, his father remarked that it almost seemed that this "subtle inner darkening began to appear physically"[5] with a darkening of his eyes and once-blonde hair.

In 1966 the boy's mother became pregnant again, and this pregnancy presented the same problems as her first. Between his father's avoidance and workaholism and his mother's nervousness and irritability, the family had no social life by the time their second child was born at the end of that year. When the boy started school, he was reluctant and fearful, seeming to dread any interactions with others and having a complete lack of self-confidence. His teacher reported that he was shy, reclusive, incredibly polite, and seemed profoundly unhappy. He didn't engage in conversation with peers and kept to himself at every possible moment. The boy's father later told authorities that his son had been abused by a neighbor when he was eight, a traumatic event that likely intensified his growing withdrawal and social unease.[4] The claim was made 22 years after the fact and denied by the boy at that time, but it aligns with behavioral patterns often seen in children who've experienced early sexual trauma, including social withdrawal, emotional detachment, and emerging signs of aggression toward animals.

Signs of emotional disturbance and anger were beginning to manifest in small ways, such as when the young boy befriended a teacher in his own way and gave her a small bowl of tadpoles as a gift. The teacher's assistant innocently gave those same tadpoles to a classmate who also happened to be the boy's neighbor and friend. The boy became enraged and, sneaking over to his neighbor's house, poured gasoline over the tadpoles to kill them. This was his first act of violence.

CHAPTER 2

Few people survive their teenage years without some major faux pas that haunt them for months. Growing into one's limbs, kicking acne to the curb, and getting over the fear of what others think is all a part of adolescence that no one reminisces longingly about. Some, however, have a bit more to work through than a few awkward encounters with unrequited crush.

From an early age the boy had a fascination with dead animals. As a young boy, his dad smelled something foul coming from under their porch and discovered rotting animal carcasses. He pulled them out and turned around to talk with his wife. When he turned back around, the young child was hitting the bones against each other and smiling, calling them "fiddlesticks." His morbid interest only increased as he got older. In May of 1968 the family moved to Ohio - their sixth move in nine years. The house stood on half an acre of wooded land, which the boy explored extensively and began to collect large insects and skeletons of small animals.[1]

A couple of years later, when it was clear to the boy's parents that his fascination wasn't going anywhere, his father decided to engage with his son's hobby by teaching him how to safely bleach and preserve the bones of animals. A chemist by trade, it was exciting for his father to bring him into his passion, just as the boy was bringing his father into his. Together they soaked the bones in a diluted bleach solution, watching the remnants of tissue dissolve until only pale, sterile fragments remained.[1]

This fascination with animals and their anatomy continued throughout high school. At around age 15, the boy made a regular habit out of riding around on his bike with a trash bag. He found dead animals along the way and scooped them into his bag, taking them home later and creating "his own private cemetery"[1] He would then strip away the flesh and bleach the bones, as his dad had taught him years previously. In one of these instances, the teenager cut off the head of a dead dog, nailed the body to a tree, and impaled the skull on a stick in the woods behind his house. He then invited a friend over to see what he had "found." The friend was, perhaps obviously, disgusted.

The teenager also grew to have that same intrigue for humans, particularly men, and their bodies. He began to recognize his attraction to men by his early teens, though he struggled to reconcile those feelings with his growing fixation on anatomy and control. It was in these young adult years that the first known instance of the teenager attempting to harm a man came when seeing an attractive man run by the same spot on a regular basis. According to his father, the teenager found it so "difficult to confront another human being"[1] that he waited for the man to pass him with plans to knock him unconscious with a baseball bat and then lie down with him. His father said that he was "becoming so afraid of other people, so intimidated by their presence, that in order for him to have contact with them, they needed to be dead."[1] When he was 15 he was assaulted by a group of kids who struck him on the back of the head with a black jack and when he fantasized about retaliating against them, it aroused him sexually.[3] More and more, this sexual arousal was driving him to turn thoughts of harming others into reality.

Meanwhile, the teenager's mother continued to unravel and with her, her marriage. Constantly ailed by constipation, insomnia, seizing episodes, and more, his mother took higher dosages of a medication called Equanil along with sleeping pills, laxatives, and valium. The doctors eventually diagnosed her condition as resulting from an "anxiety state." In 1970, the teenager's mother was checked into a psych ward at a local Ohio hospital. She was there only three days before checking herself out but then returned a few months later and stayed for a month. She eventually started group therapy and discussed openly how much she hated her father, going as far as to say she could see the face of her father superimposed over the therapist's body. Battling alcoholism his entire life, the teenager's grandfather had "wildly explosive behavior"[1] and plagued his daughter's childhood with fear and cruelty that no child should have to endure. It goes without saying that being raised in a household like that doesn't lend itself to healthy parenting techniques without very intentional healing, self-awareness, and intervention.

Throughout the entirety of the teenager's young life he experienced the bitter conflict between his parents. Between his mother's mental health issues and his father's inability to and avoidance of managing those moods, the environment was rife with tension, confusion, and emotional instability. On multiple occasions the neighbors called the police to break up fights between the two, which inevitably caused the boy and his brother anxiety at the least and severe trauma at the worst.

In a day in age where 50% of marriages end in divorce, it's not unusual for kids to experience their parents fighting. Even in the healthiest of marriages, fights happen and cruelties are spewed in moments of frustration, weakness, and fatigue. However, in homes with high conflict, children often internalize blame, thinking they were the cause of the fights or that they could have prevented them. That conflict tends to produce feelings of shame, guilt, anxiety, and confusion. Because the conflict feels unpredictable, their emotional security is out of sync and they grow hypervigilant about things like mood, silence, and cues.[2]

Children respond to emotional turmoil in the home differently; some kids withdraw and become emotionally numbed, while others may act out by showing aggression or defiance. As they get older, inner turmoil seems to deepen. The low self-esteem they get from believing their parents are fighting because of them can frequently turn into shyness in social situations, which then leads to loneliness due to difficulty initiating friendships.[2] The way parents fight is also important. If children are seeing constant fighting followed by resolution, it may mitigate some of the harm done. However, conflict followed by continued resentment, silent treatments, and more conflict furthers the harm.

For children already living in a home fraught with trauma or neglect, parental conflict is layered on top of existing wounds. What seems like a victimless crime can actually cause severe trauma and lead to psychological and behavioral issues in the moment and down the line. In the teenager's life, he experienced conflict between his parents almost from the moment he was born, followed by a traumatic hernia surgery in which the pain was so severe that he was sure his penis had been cut off. While his later sins were not his parents' fault, the things he dealt with certainly didn't help his confidence, self-esteem, or social skills.

In 1978, the fighting between the teenager's parents reached a head after his mother reportedly had an affair and then initiated a divorce. By the end of the bitter divorce, both parents had accused the other of "extreme cruelty and gross neglect of duty."[1] In the crossfire, their sons were left to absorb the fallout. The fight over custody quickly became a tug-of-war for the younger brother, while the teenager was left almost entirely out of the conversation. It was as if neither parent wanted the burden of a quiet, withdrawn teenager who no longer demanded much of anyone. When his father left and remarried and his mother moved out with his younger brother, the teenager was effectively abandoned with no food or money and with no working refrigerator.

It was later that same lonely summer that he killed his first victim.

CHAPTER 3

His whole life, the teenager struggled with his sexuality. Growing up in a conservative social climate with a staunch fundamentalist Christian father made it difficult for him to be anything but a straight, white male, and it seems likely that given his shyness and extreme social anxiety, he probably had no one to talk with about his feelings. Homosexuality was not widely accepted in the 1970s as the teenager was growing up. June 28, 1970 was the first ever gay pride parade, and "homosexuality" was still listed as a mental illness until the end of 1973.[1] His father was firmly against homosexuality and often made negative comments about gay men and lesbians. The teenager 's struggle to reconcile his desires with societal expectations likely fueled the blend of shame, repression, and control that later manifested in sexualized violence and the objectification of his victims. One of the court appointed psychiatrists in the teenager 's trial years later, Dr. Palermo, speculated that perhaps the boy was so filled with hate that in killing his victims he was actually trying to kill his own homosexuality[2].

Research on internalized homophobia shows that when individuals are taught to suppress or hate parts of their identity, that conflict doesn't disappear, it festers. Studies on intimate partner violence in same-sex relationships have found that the more shame a person feels about their sexuality, the more likely they are to direct that shame outward through control, emotional abuse, or violence. The inability to accept oneself often breeds a distorted need for dominance over others. In the boy's case, this internal battle may have taken on the form of grotesque physical actions. His attraction to men, tangled with guilt, secrecy, and fear of rejection, became inseparable from his compulsion to control, possess, and ultimately destroy.[3]

There is not much information on what happened right before this event to prompt it to occur, but what we do know is that on June 18, 1978, at 18 years old the teenager took the life of his first victim.

Night was settling over northeastern Ohio when the 18-year-old spotted a hitchhiker on the side of the road. The stranger was attractive, and on impulse, he pulled over to offer him a ride. The hitchhiker accepted, and the two seemed to connect quickly. Instead of dropping the hitchhiker off, the teenager brought him back to his home, where the encounter turned sexual. When the hitchhiker tried to leave, the teenager took a barbell and struck him in the head with it, killing him on impact. Afterward, the 18-year-old took the hitchhiker's body to a field near his family's property and proceeded to dissect it over the next couple of days, destroying the evidence[4] and eventually laying the man to rest in a nearby storm drain.[5] He wouldn't kill again for almost ten years.

In the aftermath of these events, the teenager's life began to spiral in other ways. It's not clear when he started drinking heavily, but soon he was a full-fledged alcoholic. His father came to visit one day and, when he discovered the teenager had been living alone and his mother and brother had moved out, he and his new wife moved back in to try and bring some order to the teenager's life. He enrolled the boy in college but withdrew him after only earning two college credits in the first quarter due to his failing grades. Upon coming home, the teenager was given two choices: Get a job or join the army. For several days in a row, his father drove him to the nearby mall where he could either sign up for the service or find a job at any of the numerous stores. Instead of taking a positive step toward his future, the teenager used that time to drink and ended up being jailed and charged with drunk and disorderly conduct. In 1979, the teenager joined the United States Army.[5]

The teenager's time in the army seemed to be a positive time in his life and there is no evidence that he took any other victims. Upon seeing him after his first six months in the army, his father said, "this new, completely refurbished [man] was a handsome, broad-shouldered young man who smiled brightly…I saw only positive changes that had come over him: he talked more freely, the way his eyes look at me with an unexpected openness[5]." He was in the army for the next two years and then, suddenly, was honorably discharged for alcoholism three months before his service was to be up.

The young man's alcohol addiction continued taking over his life as he moved from the army to a quick stint in Florida and then back to his father and stepmother's house. He was back to the same boy he had been before leaving for the army; he couldn't keep a job and ended up in jail again for drunk and disorderly conduct. Finally, in the early 1980s, the young man's father decided he needed a break and sent his son to his grandmother's house in Wisconsin for the weekend. It was there that the young man decided he didn't want to go back to Ohio and lived there for the next six years.[5]

The young man's time at his grandmother's was marked by positive and intentional changes in his life, or so it seemed. He helped his grandmother with housework, attended church with her, got a job as a phlebotomist, and began attending Alcoholics Anonymous. He was "mothered shamelessly" by his grandmother and was "far happier than at any time since he'd come home from the army."[5]

Throughout his stay, the young man's grandmother became increasingly concerned by some disturbing actions by her grandson. At one such time, she found a full-size department store male mannequin in his closet, dressed in a shirt and shorts. When he was confronted, he said he only stole the mannequin to prove that he could. It wasn't a crime, it was a challenge. Shortly thereafter, his grandmother started smelling disturbing odors in her home. When confronted by his father, the young man confessed that he was conducting experiments on animal carcasses but refused to let his father see what he was working on.[5]

In 1985, the young man was in the library when another man passed him a note asking him to meet him in the basement for a blow job. He turned the proposition down, but this was a linchpin moment in the young man's downward spiral. He consciously tried to suppress his urges and sought ways to satisfy them without resorting to extreme actions. For a time, these strategies seemed to work. He engaged in casual sexual encounters in bookstores and baths and explored pornography, which he used as a temporary outlet to stimulate himself. While living with his grandmother, he also experimented with Satanism and abstaining from alcohol. Yet none of these measures lasted. They were temporary fixes that never addressed the underlying issue, which, in a simplified sense, was his profoundly negative view of himself.[2]

In 1987, at age 27, the man was enjoying himself at a local gay bar when he met a stranger that he would then take to his hotel room. After getting drunk and losing consciousness, the man woke up to find the stranger in bed next to him, dead. He then took the body to his grandmother's house, where he committed acts of necrophilia, dismembered it, and disposed of the remains in the trash. This was his second murder. He was past the point of no return. Past the point of experimenting. His path was solidified.

CHAPTER 4

His name was Jeffrey Dahmer. By the time he was arrested in 1991, 17 young men were dead. For more than a decade, Dahmer moved quietly through Milwaukee's gay community, blending into bars, bathhouses, and nightclubs. Behind the calm voice and polite smile, he was luring men back to his apartment, men who would never leave alive.[1]

Before exploring the psychological and biological factors that shaped Jeffrey Dahmer, it's important to remember the real people whose lives he destroyed. Each of his victims was more than a headline or statistic, they were sons, brothers, friends, and loved ones. Their stories provide critical insight into Dahmer's evolving methods and the devastating human cost of his compulsions.

Steven Hicks was Dahmer's first victim on June 18, 1978. Hicks was a recent high-school graduate who was hitchhiking to a rock concert when Dahmer picked him up and killed him shortly thereafter. During the trial, his father described him as a caring and empathetic person, sharing a story about how he was first proud and then "cried his eyes out" after shooting his first rabbit. Nearly 10 years later, on November 20, 1987, Steven Tuomi met Dahmer in a bar and went to his hotel room with him. When Dahmer woke up, he found Tuomi dead and brought his body back to his grandmother's house with him. Tuomi was remembered as quiet but artistic and he worked as a short-order cook in Milwaukee. Tuomi was the only of Dahmer's victims that he wasn't charged for due to a lack of evidence.[2]

On January 16, 1988, fourteen-year-old Jamie Doxtator became Dahmer's next victim. Doxtator was nearly six feet tall and loved playing pool and riding his bike. He left behind his mother and three younger siblings. Just a few months later, on March 24, 1988, Dahmer met twenty-five-year-old Richard Guerrero at a bar. Guerrero's family described him as caring and responsible, the type who would always call his mother if he thought he might be in trouble. His sister later said she felt the police failed to take his disappearance seriously because of their Mexican descent. At Dahmer's trial, she called him "diablo, el puro diablo." The following year, on March 25, 1989, Dahmer killed twenty-six-year-old Anthony Sears. Sears was a rising manager at Baker's Square in Milwaukee, saving to buy an engagement ring for his girlfriend, and had ambitions of becoming a model.[2]

After almost a year, Dahmer struck again on May 20, 1990, killing thirty-three-year-old Raymond Smith, who also went by Ricky Beeks. Smith had recently been released from prison and was rebuilding his life, living with his half-sister and staying close to his ten-year-old daughter in Illinois. In June 1990, Dahmer killed twenty-eight-year-old Edward Smith, an aspiring model who was known by friends and family as loving, trusting, and respectful. Raised in a Christian home, he was remembered for his warmth and faith.[2]

That September, Dahmer met twenty-two-year-old Ernest Miller. Miller was visiting family in Milwaukee and preparing to start college to pursue his dream of becoming a professional dancer. His family remembered him as a gifted performer who had often danced at church when he was younger. Only a few weeks later, on September 24, 1990,

Dahmer met twenty-three-year-old David Thomas. Thomas left behind a two-year-old daughter, an ex-girlfriend, and a mother who still spoke lovingly of him. His ex described him as fun-loving and said she compared every man she dated to him. His mother shared that her granddaughter often sat by the window asking, "Where is Dada? When is Dada coming?"[2]

On February 18, 1991, Dahmer killed eighteen-year-old Curtis Straughter, who was known affectionately as Demetra or Curta. Straughter had recently lost his job as a nursing assistant but was determined to finish school and attend modeling classes. He was also active in Gay Youth Milwaukee and was described by his family as creative and ambitious. A few months later, on April 7, 1991, nineteen-year-old Errol Lindsey became Dahmer's next victim. Lindsey was the youngest of six children and was remembered as outgoing and playful. His sister called him a "goofball" and said he was a "mama's boy" who loved to make others laugh. He left behind a daughter born six months after his murder.[2]

On May 24, 1991, thirty-one-year-old Anthony "Tony" Hughes met Dahmer at a Milwaukee bar. Deaf and mute since infancy due to pneumonia, Hughes communicated through sign language and written notes. He was visiting family in Milwaukee from Madison at the time of his death and was remembered as intelligent, determined, and deeply loved by his community. Just three days later, on May 27, Dahmer killed fourteen-year-old Konerak Sinthasomphone. A freshman in high school, Konerak was a soccer player and the second youngest of nine children. His family, who had immigrated from Laos, was devastated by his death, particularly after learning that he might have been saved if not for police negligence. In June 1991, Dahmer met twenty-year-old Matt Turner after a gay pride parade in Chicago.

Turner was an aspiring model who had run away from home the year before and was trying to make it on his own. Friends described him as kindhearted and full of potential.[2]

Shortly afterward, on July 15th, Dahmer killed twenty-three-year-old Oliver Lacy. Lacy was a father to a two-year-old son and was engaged to be married. His mother described him as outspoken and passionate, someone who cared deeply about his loved ones. Only days later, Dahmer murdered twenty-three-year-old Jeremiah Weinberger. Originally from Puerto Rico, Weinberger worked at a video store in Chicago and was known for his creativity and attention to detail. His roommate said he "loved art and was very meticulous." Dahmer's final victim, twenty-five-year-old Joseph Bradehoft, was killed in July 1991. Bradehoft had recently moved to Milwaukee in search of work to support his wife and three children. He left home for a job interview and never returned.[2]

In most of these cases, Dahmer bludgeoned his victims, dismembered their bodies, and kept specific body parts as trophies. He also frequently dissolved other parts of the body in acid after photographing the corpses. He tried and failed to turn several of the corpses into zombies or "love slaves" by lobotomizing them and pouring acid into the hole he drilled, hoping to ensure they wouldn't leave him.

Jeffrey Dahmer was caught on July 22, 1991 and was convicted on February 15, 1992 after murdering at least 17 people. He was found to be legally sane and sentenced to 15 consecutive life terms. He was murdered in prison on November 28, 1994.

CHAPTER 5

People today are fascinated by psychopaths- particularly serial killers. They terrify us but we feel disconnected from that reality as we read about them from the safety of our home. They also offer unanswered questions: What kind of person does this? What goes through one's mind as they're brutally murdering and dismembering an innocent human being? What stops others from becoming this way? What is stopping me from becoming this way?

The answer lies in biology. Everyone is born with two amygdalae-- small, almond-shaped regions in the brain that play a crucial role in processing and regulating emotions. The amygdala's primary functions include emotional processing, memory consolidation, decision-making, social cognition, and sensory integration. When the amygdala is not working effectively, it can cause mental health or brain-related conditions such as anxiety, intermittent explosive disorder, mood disorders, PTSD, personality disorders, Alzheimer's, Autism Spectrum Disorder, brain cancer, and more.[1] Studies have found that individuals who are classified as psychopaths show significant reductions in the size and structure of both amygdalae, particularly in areas linked to emotional and social processing. These deficits may underlie the emotional detachment, lack of empathy, and antisocial behaviors that define psychopathy, suggesting that the amygdala plays a central role in its development.[2]

It is important to note that not everyone with differences in their amygdala become psychopaths and serial killers. For instance, while Jeffrey Dahmer was definitively a serial killer, he didn't show signs of psychopathy as much as Borderline Personality Disorder, Schizotypal Personality Disorder, and Sexual Paraphilias.[3]

Dr. Robert Hare created the Psychopathy Checklist (PCL) in the 1970s and it was finalized as diagnostic criteria for clinical and forensic use in 1991 as the PCL-R (Psychopathy Checklist - Revised). The PCL-R has 20 traits and behaviors that are each rated a 0 (does not manifest) to a 2 (definitely manifests); the highest score is 40, and a psychopath is designated as anyone who scores over 30. Some of the items on this test include superficial charm, grandiose sense of self-worth, proneness for boredom, pathological lying, manipulation, lack of remorse or guilt, lack of empathy, poor behavioral controls, promiscuous sexual behavior, impulsivity, failure to accept responsibility for one's own actions, and more.[4] While Dahmer certainly meets some of these qualifications (23 of 40), he is notably lacking in key areas such as superficial charm and manipulation tactics. He was incredibly shy and had very little, if any, self-confidence. He kept to himself and his primary motivation in his murders seems to have been a compulsive need to control his victims so they couldn't leave him. Unlike a textbook psychopath, Dahmer was socially awkward, lonely, felt self-hatred, had a fear of abandonment, showed some regret, and was fueled by compulsions rather than being controlled and meticulous.[3]

Dahmer's fear of abandonment, sense of emptiness, and self-hatred are what lead Forensic Psychiatrist Carl Wohlstrom to diagnose him with Borderline Personality Disorder (BPD). The DSM-5 defines BPD as a disorder characterized by a pervasive pattern of instability in relationships, self-image, and [emotions], and marked impulsivity."[7] A diagnosis requires that an individual exhibit at least five of the following: frantic efforts to avoid real or imagined abandonment; unstable and intense relationships alternating between idealization and devaluation; identity disturbance; impulsivity in at least two potentially self-damaging areas; recurrent suicidal or self-mutilating behavior; affective instability; chronic feelings of emptiness; intense or poorly controlled anger; and transient, stress-related paranoid ideation or dissociative symptoms.[7]

Some of the ways BPD manifested in Dahmer was in his fear of abandonment, impulsivity, and unstable relationships. One of the defining traits of BPD is an intense fear of being left alone. Dahmer grew up with a mentally ill mother and a largely absent father; he was abandoned at age 18 by a mother who left him and a father who remarried and didn't even know he was alone. His fear of abandonment was valid and may have been part of his severe need to control others and keep them from leaving him. By murdering his victims and engaging in necrophilia, he could ensure that they would not be the ones who would leave. On at least four different occasions he even attempted to lobotomize his victims so they would live and he could "keep" them.[6] Ultimately, Dahmer's behaviors reflected a deeply distorted attempt to cope with the fear of abandonment and emotional instability that characterize borderline personality disorder.

Another way BPD manifested in Dahmer was in his impulsivity. It was exceedingly important that Dahmer remain in control. Unlike many other known serial killers, Dahmer didn't kill with the intention of causing pain or harm to others. In his trial, he stated that he never intended to kill anyone; he just wanted to create "love slaves" or zombies that would do whatever he wanted.[8] He attempted to create these zombies by crudely lobotomizing his victims and pouring in muriatic acid.[8] This worked at first but eventually the victims died, which left him feeling disappointed at his failure.[6] In this way, his crimes can be seen as extreme manifestations of the abandonment fears, emotional dysregulation, and need for control often observed in individuals with borderline personality disorder.

Dahmer's story reminds us that even the most horrifying acts often have psychological and biological origins. Viewing him solely as a monster oversimplifies the reality of his pathology. His crimes were not born from sadistic pleasure but from desperation, compulsion, and an unrelenting need for control — all underscored by profound emotional emptiness.

PART 2

I HAD TO KILL THEM

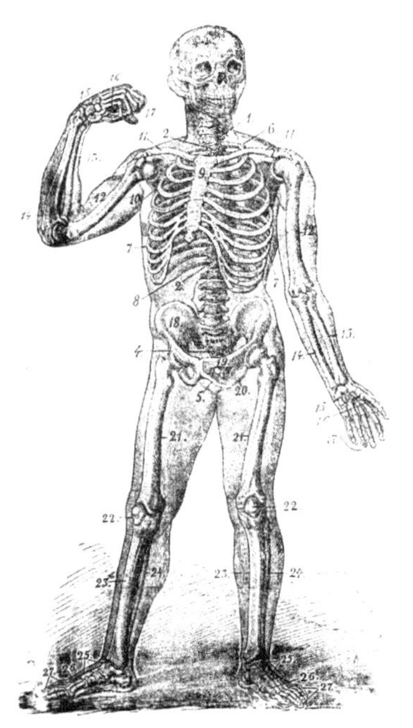

CHAPTER 6

It's a balmy afternoon in 1960s Troy, Michigan. A little girl with straight, dark hair sits on her bedroom floor, quietly dressing and undressing her dolls in the outfits her grandfather had just given her. Her older brother lies next to her, his head resting in her lap. Downstairs, her grandparents argue again, their voices rising. She knows what will happen next. No amount of hiding or locking her door will keep him from coming up the stairs and into her room.

Born into a family that made it clear they didn't want her- or, rather, only wanted her for one thing- this young girl truly didn't stand a chance. But let's back up to the very beginning and you'll see why some commenters on forums such as Reddit have said things like, "This is the only serial killer I actually feel bad for."

The girl was born on February 29, 1956 in Rochester, Michigan to a 16-year-old mother and a schizophrenic father who was imprisoned for kidnapping and raping a 7-year-old child. Seconds old and already the cards were stacked against her. By the time she was 4 years old, she'd been abandoned at her grandparents' house when her mother dropped her and her brother off and never came back.[5]

Life at her grandparents' was good- at first. Her grandmother was the first true mother figure she'd had in her life, and it's easy to assume she was happy with her life for the first time in her four years of existence. According to her best friend, her grandmother dressed her in beautiful clothes, fed her well, and kept the house clean.[5] It was a far stretch from the time spent with her alcoholic mother who, in the girl's first ever memory of her mother told her, "I tried to abort you but I failed."[5]

Parental abandonment during the earliest years, like what this girl experienced when her father was absent before she was born and her mother left by age four, can have profound and lasting effects on a child's brain development and emotional health. Neuroscientific research[2] shows that when young children do not receive consistent, responsive caregiving—what the brain expects during early "serve and return" interactions—neural circuits fail to form as they should. This affects brain regions responsible for emotional regulation, impulse control, attention, and stress resilience, such as the prefrontal cortex, amygdala, and anterior cingulate. Children raised without reliable caregivers often show reduced brain activity, weaker neural connections, and smaller or underdeveloped areas linked to emotional and social processing. Essentially, the brain's foundation is built on instability.

Beyond structure, their stress systems also become dysregulated. Neglected children frequently show irregular cortisol patterns, meaning their bodies may stay in a heightened or blunted state of stress even when no threat exists. The result is often chronic physiological stress, emotional reactivity, and difficulty calming down or forming secure attachments. Over time, this impacts how they process emotions, make decisions, and relate to others. These children are at higher risk for anxiety, depression, and poor impulse control, which can make it hard to trust or connect with people later in life. For someone like this girl, whose earliest experiences lacked safety and attunement, this kind of developmental disruption helps explain why her adult relationships, emotional regulation, and worldview were shaped by deep-seated instability and mistrust.[2]

Research shows more specifically that early maternal rejection is linked to future violent behavior.[5] After hypothesizing that birth complications combined with early maternal rejection led to adult violent crime, one study found that the combination of those two risk factors had a much higher likelihood of becoming violent in adulthood. The study "indicated that those who experienced both high birth complications and early child rejection were most likely to become violent criminals, i.e., of offenders who had both risk factors, 47.2% became violent compared with only 19.7% of offenders who had neither risk factor or only one."[3] There is very little information about the girl's birth, but in an interview with her mother, she said the girl was a "frank breech birth," which would qualify as a birth complication in the context of the study. Combined with the early maternal abandonment she experienced, this suggests that she was exposed to both risk factors identified in the research, potentially increasing her vulnerability to later behavioral and emotional difficulties.

The one silver lining of the girl's abandonment by her mother was the love she received from her grandmother. Though ineffectual, it was the most love she had ever received. Her grandfather, however, was a different story. While living with her grandparents, the girl was regularly physically abused by her grandfather. Her friend described a time when she was driving past the girl's house and saw her being beaten by him.[1] Another time, that same friend shared that the two had skipped school and "...the minute she walked in [to her house], [her grandfather] had her over a chair and … he beat the hell out of her with a black belt that was around his waist… and he walloped on her for a good 5 minutes."[1] When she was 7 years old, she didn't eat her baked potato at dinner so her grandfather forced her to fish the potato out of the trash and eat it; he then stripped her from the waist down and beat her so badly she wasn't able to go to school the next day.[4] While the girl's grandmother wanted to care for her and her brother, her grandfather resented the kids and associated them with their promiscuous mother.[4] He told her she was worthless, wicked, unwanted from the start, and that she "should never have been born."[4]

There were also indications that the girl was sexually abused by her grandfather. During his vicious "spankings," he would strip her down, make her bend over the kitchen table, and smack her with a leather belt. He would also make her "lay face down, spread-eagle and naked on the bed for whippings."[4] She recounted to a friend that when she was in her early teens she had sex with her grandfather; she also said that at one point her grandfather grabbed her in front of her grandmother, kissed her on the mouth, and forced his tongue down her throat.[4]

This abuse, coupled with the early abandonment by her mother and the absence of her father, left the girl without a stable source of care or protection during the formative years of her life. The constant fear, humiliation, and betrayal eroded her sense of safety and trust, shaping a worldview in which adults were dangerous and unreliable. Even as a child, she began to develop coping mechanisms that prioritized survival over emotional connection, a pattern that would carry into her adolescence. The cumulative trauma of neglect, physical punishment, and sexual abuse created deep psychological scars, laying the groundwork for the challenges and behaviors that would emerge in her teenage years.

CHAPTER 7

In letters she wrote to her best friend from prison, the girl shares that while the first time she had sex was around age nine with her brother ("it was all mutual"[1]), the first time she was ever raped was at age 13.[1] She was at a party and when she awoke she found herself tied to a bed being gang-raped. According to her letters, this happened "at least" three more times in the same year. Her final rape in that time period came at age 14 when she was hitchhiking home from a party about eight miles away. The man who picked her up said he knew her "father" (her grandfather) and where she lived, so the teenager felt comfortable accepting a ride from him. The events that transpired were "too embarrassing" for the teenager to get into details about with her friend, but she ended up pregnant.[1] Unsurprisingly, her grandfather told her it was her fault.[2] The teenager successfully hid her pregnancy from the public for six months, but was then sent to a home for unwed mothers in Detroit. There, she gave birth to a "huge" child (she couldn't remember if he was 7lbs 11oz or 11lbs 7oz.)[1]

Shortly after the teenager had given up her son for adoption and returned home, she ran away due to her grandfather's continued physical abuse.[2] When her grandmother died of a liver disorder, it seemed to the teenager that the last person in the world who loved her was now gone. She was alone again.

Right around when the news got to the now-15-year-old that her grandmother had died, the cops found her and took her to a juvenile center. She ran away a week or two later and, after running and partying for three weeks, she was "busted" and then promptly sent to a Girls' Training School in Adrian, Michigan.[1] The teenager tried and failed to run away from the Girls' home several times and was finally told that if she didn't attempt to escape anymore for 60 days, she could leave. She agreed, and 60 days later she was let go.[1]

Newly homeless as her grandfather refused to let her live at his house, the teenager lived on the streets or in the woods behind her house. She curried favor with others by offering sex and sexual favors in return for food and cigarettes (something she denies in her letters[1] but is corroborated by multiple sources). Her friend Dawn, to whom she wrote letters to all those years later, described how the teenager survived by bathing in the lake and finding food in the nearby woods known as "the pits." Despite everything, she still went to school, sneaking into gas stations to wash her hair and clothes. None of her classmates or their families would take her in, so she sometimes slept in abandoned cars behind a large house in town. "People called her names-bitch, slut, whore, ugly bitch, and 'Cigarette Pig' (because she smoked at an early age and because she was willing to give sexual favors to boys in exchange for cigarettes)."[2] One of the people who let her stay at his house was a high school peer who got her drunk and high, and then invited his friends over to gang rape her. When she threatened to call the cops, her perpetrators said they'd kill her if she did.[1]

In 1976 when the young woman was 20 years old, she met a 69-year-old yacht club president and the two were married soon after. Their love affair was short-lived, however, as he filed a restraining order against her for assault within the first several weeks of their marriage. According to her, he was "sexually perverted" and she "grabbed a 22 rifle, threw him on the floor, put [her] foot on his chest and the barrel of the rifle to his forehead, and said, 'I want a divorce within 24 hours or I'll kill you.'"[1] After divorcing her husband, the young woman drifted into a chaotic lifestyle marked by prostitution, drinking, and constant partying. She often used hitchhiking as a way to find clients, flagging down men on the road and then offering sex in exchange for money as a means of survival.[1] As a prostitute, she was often victimized by her clients, and was frequently raped and even left for dead after the fact. Over the next few years, her actions grew more desperate. One night, she held up a convenience store, stealing thirty-five dollars and a pack of cigarettes. She was later charged with robbery with a deadly weapon and sentenced to three years in prison.

The woman "started the gay scene at 28"[1] and her first relationship lasted about a year with a woman named Toni. After they broke up, she met Tyria and dated her for about four years. In the woman's own words, "One of the reasons I loved her so – was for her down-to-earth ways and honesty."[1] She and Tyria lived together starting from mere weeks after they met. According to Dawn, the woman loved Tyria with "her whole heart soul and mind" but Tyria may have only loved her "with her heart."[4] In the woman's words, though, "It was all in a 'sisterly sense,' with no interest in the sex part. No way. It was against the grain of nature for me and God. So all my love leaned more towards just pure friendship."[1] She supported Tyria by continuing to work as a prostitute so the two would be financially secure, and that's when the real drama started.

Knowing her career was high-risk, the woman was concerned that if she got into trouble with the law she would never see Tyria again. With this in mind, she decided to steal a gun and keep it with her just in case anyone tried to mess with her while she was working. She and Tyria were allegedly picked on by others for being gay and were thrown out of their apartment on more than one occasion due to prejudice on the part of the landlord. The woman also claimed a neighbor kidnapped and killed one of their pets "only because they found out we were gay."[1]

The more they ran into instances like these, the angrier the woman became. With evictions continuing and rent getting more and more expensive in places that would accept the couple, they found themselves in need of higher paying jobs. Tyria got a job as a laundry worker at a hotel but only made $300 every other week, so it was decided that the woman had to make $1500 across three days or they would get evicted from yet another apartment. Unfortunately, it was rainy season, which meant the clients were lacking and the woman was only able to bring home $80/day on rainy days or about $300/day when the sun shone.[1]

It was late at night after a hard day of trying and only somewhat succeeding at making money for herself and Tyria. The woman was exhausted, missed her girlfriend desperately, and wanted to get home to her as quickly as possible. Trying to move things along, the woman decided to hitchhike her way home later than usual, despite knowing the risks that came with doing so. Around 10:30pm a car slowed down and a man named Richard Mallory rolled down his window and asked if she wanted a ride.[1]

Less than one hour later Mallory was dead and the woman's life was forever changed.

CHAPTER 8

Although other women have been convicted for murder, many view Aileen Wuornos as a uniquely predatory female serial killer, due to the nature and pattern of her crimes. However, it's certainly easy for the reader to see why there are people who feel sorry for her or don't think she was given a fair chance in life. Her upbringing was traumatic and she was traumatized over and over again throughout her early adulthood as well. In interviews with the police she repeatedly said she never planned to kill anybody but did so as self-defense: "I had no intentions of killing anybody ... it wasn't intentional killing. It wasn't just kill somebody. It was because they physically attacked me…. I mean I had to kill 'em--or it's retaliation, too. It's like, you bastards. You were gonna-you were gonna hurt me."[1]

Aileen claimed she killed Richard Mallory on December 1, 1989 after he allegedly violently raped her. In one recollection to the police, she said she knew he was going to rape her so she held him up at gun point and then shot him while he was still in the car. In another version, she said he had violently raped her and then threatened to kill her "like the other sluts I've done" and telling her, once she started struggling, "You're dead, bitch. You're dead."[2]

On June 1, 1990, David Spears, a construction worker, was found along the interstate after Aileen purportedly shot him multiple times with her .22. Just a few days later, June 6, 1990, the body of part-time rodeo worker Charles Carskaddon was found after being shot nine times. Peter Siems was never found but his car was discovered on July 4, 1990, nearly a month after he was reported missing; Aileen confessed to killing him and witnesses identified Tyria and Aileen as leaving the scene of the crime. The body of Troy Burress, a salesman, was severely decomposed by the time it was found on August 4, 1990, and the police don't know his exact date of death. Dick Humphreys, a retired Air Force major and police chief, was murdered by Aileen on September 11, 1990 and found the following day. Aileen's final victim, Walter Antonio, was discovered November 19, 1990.[2]

In each of these instances, Aileen said that she waited on the highway until someone stopped and offered her a ride. She would then admit that she was a prostitute and offer herself in exchange for alcohol, marijuana, other drugs, or money. After some foreplay and as the men were stripping off their clothes, Aileen "exited the car's passenger side, taking her belongings with her. When the victims sensed danger, Aileen would shoot and kill them. Typically, she would scream at her companions, alleging that "I knew you were going to rape me!"[4]

When asked why she killed these men, Aileen repeatedly framed the killings as acts of self-defense, saying that after years of being raped and abused she refused to be beaten or raped and would shoot men who got violent with her. "I killed 'em because they got violent with me and I decided to defend myself. I wasn't gonna let 'em beat the shit outta me or kill me, either."[1] Her language about how many men she'd encountered is inconsistent, she alternately claimed figures like 250,000 and 100,000, which reads as both exaggeration and a sign of her intoxicated, traumatized state.

In her statement she admits to being drunk much of the time, says she carried a weapon in plain view, and explains she shot men she felt would harm her or later report her. That explanation is her account and reflects her fear, anger, and guilt, but it is not a justification for the killings.[1]

While some of these men had criminal records, they were for the most part normal men with jobs and families. Did they attempt to rape Aileen? That's something no one will ever know for certain. But one thing is for sure, no matter what those men did, they had the right to a fair trial, just like Aileen did. By killing them outside the bounds of law, she took away that freedom and in doing so took her own away as well.

CHAPTER 9

Unfortunately, Aileen isn't the only girl who had a tragic and traumatic upbringing involving abuse, rape, and a lack of love. So why did she become one of America's most notorious female killers?

The domino that started the chain reaction was Aileen's father– Leo Pittman. Pittman was a diagnosed schizophrenic and a convicted child molester who was charged with kidnapping and raping a 7-year-old. While Aileen never met her father, she had his blood running through her veins, so genetics certainly play a part. Generically speaking, genes are like the blueprints that tell our bodies and brains how to develop. When traits are dominant, only one parent needs to have that trait for it to develop in the child. When traits are recessive, the trait must show up in both parents for it to appear in the child. With mental illnesses, genetics play a part but whether the risk turns into a genetic disorder also depends on life experiences, upbringing, and environment. Schizophrenia doesn't come from just one gene, but many different genes, each contributes a small amount of risk. If one parent is diagnosed with schizophrenia, that might mean the child will also be diagnosed with schizophrenia or a related mental illness, but it also might not. It certainly increases the child's odds but doesn't guarantee they'll have it. Often, mental illness in general runs in families because the multiple genetic risks are passed down *and* the environment and upbringing is less stable due to that mental illness.[2]

While schizophrenia itself is passed down through genetic traits, personality disorders originate in early childhood and are the result of both environmental and genetic traits. "Personality disorders are not simple or direct consequences of bad parenting or child abuse but are rooted in interactions between an abnormal temperament (usually considered to be genetically fixed) and an adverse environment."[4] In Aileen's case, the combination of her genetics and her traumatic childhood created the perfect storm for her eventual diagnosis of Borderline Personality Disorder and Antisocial Personality Disorder.[3]

Characterizations of Borderline Personality Disorder (BPD) include emotional, interpersonal, and behavioral dysfunctions. The disorder affects about 0.5%-5.9% of the population and is equally impacted by both genetics and environment (heritability = 35-69%).[4] Individuals with BPD often experience intense and rapidly shifting emotions, unstable relationships, and a fragile sense of self. They may struggle with impulsivity, fear of abandonment, and extreme reactions to perceived rejection or loss. Many also experience chronic feelings of emptiness, difficulty regulating anger, and cycles of idealizing and devaluing others. When combined with genetic vulnerability, traumatic experiences such as sexual violence or emotional abuse in childhood can trigger symptoms of BPD.[4] Aileen was abandoned over and over again throughout her childhood and would understandably have been fearful of abandonment. That fear of abandonment played out in her aggression toward other ones, including her loved ones. She was also extremely impulsive and admitted that none of her murders were premeditated but were results of alcohol and attempted rape.[5]

Antisocial Personality Disorder (ASPD) is characterized by a persistent disregard for social norms and violation of others' rights. They may be impulsive, manipulative, and lack empathy or remorse, sometimes engaging in deceitful or risky behaviors without concern for consequences.[4] While Aileen was diagnosed with ASPD before her trial, her apology to the police doesn't fit with this lack of remorse that is commonplace among those with ASPD:

"I'm very sorry about this. I didn't mean to do what I did. I just - I don't think I knew what I was doing ... I'm a good person inside but when I get drunk I don't know what happens when somebody messes with me .... When somebody hassles me, I mean, I'm like, don't fuck with me ... I never woulda hurt anybody unless I had to and I had to at the time ...."[5]

This contradiction highlights the complexity of Aileen's psychological profile. While her actions and diagnosis align with traits of ASPD, her statements and behaviors suggest that her emotional experiences and motivations may not fit neatly within that label. It's possible that trauma, instability, and environmental factors played a significant role in shaping her behavior, making her case far more nuanced than a single diagnosis can explain.

When it comes to specifics of Aileen's psychology in regard to her upbringing and the environment she was raised in, it's been made abundantly clear that there was little chance for her to have a "normal" life. Dr. Jethro Toomer is a forensic and clinical psychologist who conducted a psychological assessment of Aileen before her trial. In an interview he did with criminal psychologist Dr. Michelle Ward, he shared that it would have been nearly impossible for Aileen to have come out of her childhood unscathed. Not only was she predisposed to schizophrenia due to her father having it, but she was also abused and neglected almost from day one. Safety, stability, and predictability are crucial for a healthy foundation and Aileen didn't have any of those. Her foundation was constantly shifting. She learned from an early age that she couldn't trust anyone, and her primary question became "How do I survive?"[1]

Maslow's Hierarchy of Needs says that in order to move upwards through the hierarchy, one must have all the needs met in each of the lower levels: first physiological needs, then safety and security, then love and belonging, self-esteem, and finally self-actualization. Aileen Wuornos didn't even have that lowest level– food and shelter– met. From a young age she learned that having sex with men was how she would get those needs met. In an interview,[1] Psychologist Dr. Tasha Jackson shared that "when it comes to trauma, often we put ourselves back in that place of trauma and try to reframe it." She went on to explain that this is often a way that people try to heal themselves from old trauma. Perhaps in prostituting herself Aileen was trying to reframe her early childhood belief that all men are bad and, in turn, heal herself from those early traumatic experiences. One study found that children who were abused or neglected were twice as likely to engage in prostitution as adults, and this may be because these victims use sexuality as a means of building and securing relationships, affection, or material needs.[6]

From an attachment perspective, Aileen's internal narrative was shaped by repeated betrayal, neglect, and abuse. The people who were supposed to love and protect her instead became the very source of her pain. As a result, she learned four powerful, destructive lessons about herself and the world: that she was unworthy of love, that love brought harm, that life was dangerous and unpredictable, and that trust was a liability. This kind of early learning rewires a person's sense of safety and belonging. When a child grows up believing that love equals pain, they begin to anticipate rejection before it even happens.[7] Hypervigilance becomes a survival skill. Aggression becomes a form of self-protection.

Aileen's adult behaviors can be viewed through that lens. When she sold sex, she wasn't just exchanging her body for money or survival. She was reenacting her earliest lessons about connection, power, and safety. Except this time, she was the one in control. By choosing when, where, and with whom, she may have been trying to reclaim agency in a dynamic that had once left her powerless. This doesn't make her actions justified, but it does make them understandable. Trauma often pushes people to replay their past in an attempt to rewrite it, even if that rewriting takes place in ways that are destructive or self-sabotaging.

At its core, trauma is the disruption of safety and trust. The brain's job is to restore that balance, and when it can't do so through healthy means, it improvises. For Aileen, the combination of genetic predisposition, environmental chaos, and the repeated reinforcement that love and safety were conditional created a fractured sense of identity. Every violent act, every impulsive decision, every moment of rage was an echo of that foundation. Her life became a tragic case study in how unhealed trauma, left unaddressed, can evolve into something far more dangerous.

Aileen Wuornos wasn't born evil. She was born into chaos. Her genetics may have lit the match, but her environment poured the gasoline. Without intervention, love, or consistent safety, the line between survival and destruction blurred. And when a person's entire worldview is built on fear, betrayal, and mistrust, even acts of violence can feel, in their mind, like self-defense.

PART 3

LUCIFER DWELLS
IN US ALL

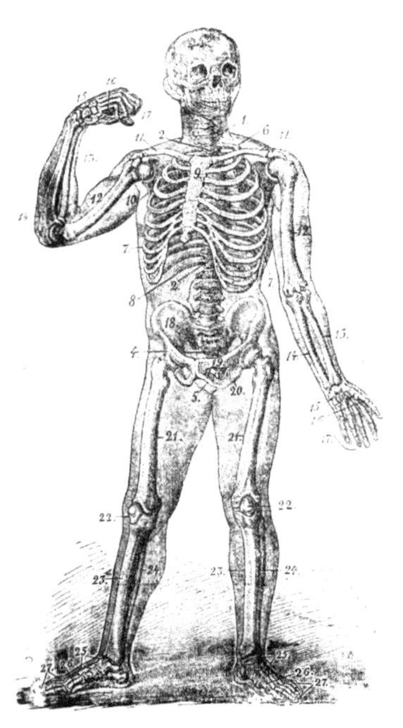

CHAPTER 10

It's a hot day in Northern Mexico in the 1920s and the sun is beating down on the clay tiles of the house, making the inside feel like an oven with no relief. A young boy is walking slowly up the driveway with a failed math test in his right hand, dragging his feet as he anticipates the beating he will get for the poor grade. As he walks inside, his father looks at him expectantly. Avoiding eye contact, the boy places the test on the table. Out of the corner of his eye, he sees his father's face turn a dark, crimson shade of red, the color it only turns right before the worst of the beatings. The boy whimpers and closes his eyes, awaiting his punishment.

Beyond the walls of that small home, the family's story was unfolding against a backdrop of events far greater than they could have imagined. At the time of the family's establishment, they were living in Mexico about 200 miles from where the U.S. government was conducting nuclear bomb tests and while there were rumors about the testing causing birth defects, it wasn't confirmed or publicized yet. Later, it was found that exposure to radioactive fallout from nuclear weapons testing led to measurable human health effects, particularly increased rates of thyroid cancer and other radiation-related diseases. Research has also shown that radioactive contamination entered the food chain and environment, which exposed nearby populations to radiation that could contribute to genetic damage and developmental effects in unborn children.[1]

The family's first child was born in the early 1950s with lumps all over his body. He was very sick and it was not believed that he would live. After praying over their son and having a minister give him his last rites two separate times, the child began to get better. Two months later, the couple fell pregnant again and were blessed with a healthy baby boy. Six months later, though, he began crying frequently as though he was in great pain. When he was one year old, he was diagnosed with Collier's disease, which was causing his bones to curve as they grew. The child was severely handicapped and was facing a lifetime of surgical operations. It was around this time that his parents realized the effects of the nuclear bomb testing[3].

In the Spring of 1954, the family moved to the safer and cleaner city of El Paso so the children could be raised in the United States. There, the couple had two more relatively healthy babies over the next two years - a boy and a girl. During this time, the children's mother started working at a boot making factory where she would mix pigments and chemicals for the boots. Due to the toxicity of the chemicals- benzene, toluene, and xylene- she should have worn a mask while working, but one was not provided to her. She found that she started getting dizzy spells and had to sit down often; the weekends were the worst, as she felt anxious and irritable until she went back to work on Monday. She, along with her sister who also worked there, began to suspect she was addicted to the chemicals but did not seek out medical attention[3].

This is another one of those instances when research later showed how much damage exposure to chemicals and other dangerous substances had on people who didn't know any better. Studies have shown that the presence of benzene, toluene, and xylene have a substantially negative effect on human health. Not only that, but being that the boy's mother likely worked inside, she was as little as two to five times and as much as 100 times more impacted by the chemical pollution than had she been outside. Benzene is the most dangerous of the three and has been shown to increase the chances of leukemia and aplastic anemia.[2] All this to say, the boy's mother was in an incredibly perilous situation and there's no telling the effects that exposure had on her own health and the health of her future children.

On February 29, 1960 in El Paso, the couple had one more baby- the antagonist of our story- and their family was complete. This pregnancy was by far the most difficult, as his mother was frequently sick from the effects of the chemicals. Due to the toxicity of the chemicals she was at that point addicted to, the doctor believed that her body was attempting to reject the child and told her she needed to quit her job, so she did. Soon after, she gave birth to her fifth child.[3]

The kids' father had a temper and would frequently punish them for "misbehaving" by physical means. When one of his older sons brought him a bad report card, he whipped him with a water hose. In 1963, their father was so enraged by his own failure to fix a mechanical issue, that he bashed his head against the side of the house until there was blood running down his face. Unfortunately, all the kids had learning disabilities, low IQs, or were simply below-average students, and no amount of punishment or beatings from their father would improve their standings at school. Their father was even-tempered most of the time and mostly kept to himself, but when he felt let down or disrespected, he lost his temper and the whole house felt it. One example of this behavior is when one of his sons was arrested for stealing a car. His father saw red and beat his son mercilessly until he was black and blue all over. This happened more than once as his son continued getting in trouble with the law. "His anger was so bad it became a kind of unspoken dread that lurked around the house at all times."[3] While it may have started as corporal punishment, it quickly turned into physical abuse.

The boy's early childhood was fairly typical. He played with his siblings, was fiercely protected by his only sister, got his fair share of cuts, bruises, and stitches, and had a wild imagination. When he started school, he started having "grand mal" epileptic episodes and was diagnosed with epilepsy, but the doctor told his parents he would "grow out of it" and did not provide them with any medication or ask to see him back. However, his family noticed that he would have long spells of staring off into space one to two dozen times per month until his early teens; they didn't know at the time that these were petit mal seizures or "absent" seizures[3].

As he got older, his seizures began to look different, and he was eventually diagnosed with temporal lobe epilepsy, a type of epilepsy that affects the parts of the brain involved in emotion and behavior. Studies[4] have shown that people with this form of epilepsy can experience changes in personality or mood, including irritability, sudden anger, or even violent outbursts. Most people with epilepsy are not aggressive, but researchers have found that when the areas of the brain that help control emotions misfire, it can sometimes trigger intense rage or confusion during or after seizures. In more severe cases, these episodes can lead to brief periods of disorientation or psychosis, especially after multiple seizures in a short time.

When the boy was seven or eight years old, his older brother was placed in a class in his middle school that was for children with learning disabilities. His teacher, Mr. McMan, was "an obsessed child molester who, over the years, sexually abused dozens of kids who'd passed through his class."[3] McMan abused two of the boy's older brothers but they never told anyone because, though they knew it was wrong, it felt good and they wanted to stay on the teacher's good side. Later, when asked if their little brother had been abused, both brothers said they didn't know but that the boy had been alone with McMan many times. When the boy was asked, he said he didn't remember.

By the time he turned ten, his life was already being shaped by things he had no control over. Poverty, illness, and trauma were constant, quietly leaving deep marks on his growing mind. His seizures went untreated, his family was weighed down by loss and disability, and the adults who should have kept him safe often became sources of fear and confusion. Whether it was the effects of his epilepsy, the instability at home, or the wounds left by abuse, the foundation for something dark was being laid long before anyone noticed.

CHAPTER 11

The boy was around 12 years old when his cousin Mike came home from Vietnam after two tours, a war hero. Mike quickly took the boy under his wing and began telling him all the grisly details of his life in the war, including how he killed at least 29 people and raped many women. He told the boy, "Having power over life and death was an incredible rush. It was godlike. You controlled who'd live and who died- you were God."[1] He showed the boy photos of women with guns to their heads giving him oral sex and told him the stories in graphic detail. In an interview later in his life, the boy said, "He tore off their clothes and had them naked tied to a tree… he cut off their heads."[1] Instead of being disgusted by this behavior, the boy was intrigued and turned on by the stories. Mike also taught the boy "how to use a knife, where to shoot someone, how to be invisible at night…"[1] To the boy, Mike was a god. While he knew Jesus would look down upon these things, "Satan would have approved of the thoughts and feelings he was having, and he started to think maybe Satan would be a more appropriate god… for him to follow and worship."[1]

In 1973 the 12-year-old witnessed Mike kill his wife in cold blood. They were at Mike's house playing pool and smoking pot when his wife came in the house and immediately started complaining about not having enough money and Mike not having a job. Mike told her to "shut up" and to stop her "complaining, whining bullshit." When she wouldn't stop, he took his gun and threatened to kill her if she didn't stop talking. She dared him to shoot her and he took her up on that dare, shooting her in the face point-blank.[1]

After this incident, the boy seemed to lose what interest he had left in school and anything productive, instead becoming more intrigued by getting high and criminal activity such as stealing. "He loved the feeling of being in a stranger's house when they weren't there, alone, looking through their personal things, taking what he wanted, fantasizing about sexual scenarios involving bondage. It gave him power."[1] He became addicted to drugs like LSD, rarely went to school, and began thinking of Satan as a close friend whom he could tell all his closest secrets to.

Around this time the teenager's father told the 15-year-old that if he wasn't going to take school seriously he may as well get a job. He started working with his older brother at a butcher shop but quit after nearly cutting off his thumb. Shortly after, he found a position at a hotel doing maintenance work and housecleaning. It was here that he became even more obsessed with women and sex, masturbating frequently while imagining scenarios with various women around the hotel. He would also go to the hotel on nights he didn't work and look through the cracks in the blinds, watching women as they undressed and imagining more and more vicious scenes involving bondage and rape. After working there for about three months, he managed to gain access to a master hotel key and worked his way up to entering rooms and stealing valuable items.

After engaging in these behaviors for some time, they stopped fulfilling the teenager and he needed more, so he devised a plan to break into a room and take a woman for himself. The first woman he tried this with was in her late twenties. Her husband had stepped out to get food when the boy entered, tied her up, pulled off her clothes, and attempted to have sex with her. Before the teenager was able to rape her, the woman's husband came back and attacked the 5'10 120lb teenager, beating him up and knocking him unconscious. The teenager went to the hospital and was detained overnight, but the couple wanted to forget the attempted rape had ever happened, so they refused to testify and the teenager was never punished for his actions.[1]

Having grown up Christian, the teenager's mind and heart constantly warred between what he saw as two counterparts: Jesus and Satan. He saw Jesus as representing good and Satan as representing evil, and he believed that while Jesus would scorn him for his thoughts and actions, Satan would embrace him.[1] Eventually the teenager became addicted to cocaine, which muddled his brain even more, drawing him further from Jesus and closer to Satan and sadistic thoughts and acts. His obsession with the idea of Satan didn't stay abstract for long. He started digging into what Satanism really was and found himself pulled in by the darkness it promised.

The religion of "Satansim" comes from the worship of Satan, an angel from the Christian bible who rebelled against God. Allegations of Satanism or "devil worship" often went hand-in-hand with witchcraft, incestuous sexual orgies, cannibalistic infanticide, and child sacrifice. In the 1980s and 1990s a book about a woman who remembered being abused in satanic rituals as a child was published and treated as fact, causing widespread panic. This cultural phenomenon was known as "Satanic Panic" and people became convinced that organized, underground satanic cults were secretly abusing children, conducting human sacrifices, and infiltrating schools and daycares. Most, if not all, of this panic was due to "recovered memories" from people who had been allegedly abused in satanic rituals. The panic ended in the mid-1990s when more research came out about faulty memories and how easily suggestion could create entirely false recollections. The FBI also released reports confirming there was no evidence of organized satanic ritual abuse in the U.S.[2]

Modern Satanists generally fall into two main groups: those who see Satan or Lucifer as a symbol (atheistic satanists) representing ideals like freedom, reason, and individuality, and those who view Satan or Lucifer as a real spiritual being (theistic satanists) and choose to worship or honor him directly. Atheistic Satanists reject supernatural beliefs altogether, using Satan as a metaphor for questioning authority and embracing one's own power and responsibility. Theistic Satanists, on the other hand, often see Satan as a bringer of knowledge and liberation rather than an embodiment of evil. Based on his statements and behavior, the teenager was most likely a theistic Satanist, as he spoke about Satan as someone who embodied evil and power. He didn't use Satan as a metaphor for rebellion or independence the way atheistic Satanists do; instead, he saw him as a real force who accepted him when he felt condemned by Jesus and traditional morality. His statements during and after his crimes show that he viewed Satan as both a companion and a source of justification for his violence.[2]

Research[3] has found that people with stronger psychopathic traits are more likely to get involved in things like dark rituals, black magic, or joining occult groups. The research suggested that those with a mix of coldness, impulsivity, and emotional emptiness might be drawn to satanism because it gives them a sense of power or control that they can't find anywhere else. In other words, the same traits that make someone manipulative or detached might also pull them toward belief systems that glorify rebellion and dominance. When looking at the teenager's childhood, it makes sense that he was pulled toward the sense of control he got from satanism. Having grown up Christian but knowing his desires were less-than-Christ-like, he naturally switched directions and started walking toward the being that would embrace him rather than push him to change his ways.

CHAPTER 12

It was 1977 and the teenager was still in Texas but living with his sister. His cousin, Mike, had been released from the mental hospital just four and a half years after killing his wife because the doctors there believed he had been fully rehabilitated. Mike believed "only the strong survived, and he took it upon himself to make [the teenager] strong"[1] by giving him even more graphic details of his conquests in Vietnam and teaching him how to do the same. Unfortunately, the teenager's cousin wasn't the only one who carried stories like this home from Vietnam. Atrocities weren't rare. In some units, they were routine, and men were told outright that brutality was expected. One soldier later testified that their commanders ordered them to "kill anything that moved." On March 16, 1968, several battalions entered a Vietnamese community called My Lai expecting enemy fire but finding only civilians going about their day. Women cooking breakfast. Children tending animals. Elderly men sweeping their yards. None of it mattered. Civilians were rounded up and, under direct orders, executed. Mothers were shot while holding their babies. Entire families were forced into ditches before the men opened fire. Some soldiers raped the women and girls first. Homes were burned to the ground. Livestock were slaughtered for no reason other than destruction for destruction's sake. When investigators finally uncovered what happened, the estimates showed that three to five hundred civilians were murdered that day. And for many of the men involved, this wasn't treated as a horrifying aberration. It was just another mission.[2]

Based on the warped moral construct the teenager and his family were living in, it's not surprising that his cousin's stories of normalized wartime behavior had such an impact on him. They didn't seem way out of left field, just maybe slightly out of bounds. But an "out of bounds" that was sure to be encouraged by his dear Lord and friend, Satan.

Around the same time his cousin was released from prison, the teenager began burglarizing people's homes and soon became known as "fingers" because if it wasn't nailed down, he would take it. Based on his nickname and behaviors, it's likely that he surrounded himself with likeminded individuals who also engaged in similar activities and encouraged him in his wayward ways. While he enjoyed the rush of breaking, entering, and stealing, it got to be a little monotonous and he dreamt of moving to Los Angeles, where he had visited his older brother several times.

By the following year the young man's dream to move to Los Angeles came true and he was able to up his burglarizing game, calling it his "career." He used the money he earned from this "job" to buy drugs, which was another common occurrence in those days. The 1970s in LA saw the shift from drugs like marijuana and LSD to harder drugs like cocaine. In order to combat this shift, the US government established the Drug Enforcement Administration (DEA) in 1973, but by then it just may have been too late. Hollywood being the center of all things creative, cocaine was the glamorous drug all the creatives were doing to stay awake and keep their minds alive. When asked to think back about that time, one "skilled craftsman" said to a New York Times writer in 1978, "Whenever I went to talk to the producer, I didn't know if I was dealing with someone on Valium, someone on bennies, someone who had just been snorting coke or a rational human being."[3]

Within a year and a half of living in LA, the young man was hot-wiring and stealing cars and then living out of those cars for a few days at a time before finding his next car. He also began studying maps of LA and seeking out neighborhoods with more expensive homes that he could burglarize. He saw himself as a Robinhood of sorts, stealing from the rich and giving to the… well, to himself. He started using and selling PCP as the "angel dust" became more and more popular. One night in 1978, a woman approached him about finding PCP to smoke. The young man gave her some, and in turn she took him back to her apartment so they could get stoned together. When the young man tried putting the moves on the woman, she rejected him and told him she was a lesbian. This angered him and later that night, after he supposedly went home for the night, he snuck back into her house to take what he thought he deserved. The young man gagged her, tied her up, ripped off her clothes, and raped her multiple times.[1]

Shortly after this first act of brutality, the young man dove even deeper into the world of Satanism. He discovered a book called "The Satanic Bible" and, after stealing a car, drove to San Francisco to meet the author, Anton LaVey. In LaVey's organization, there were no rules. There was no such thing as "sin" or "guilt" and his followers could follow their every whim while remaining blameless in his eyes. The young man quickly adopted this view and saw LaVey as a holy figure. He attended a ceremony of LaVey's and told his mom later, "I was touched by Satan tonight, he came to me."[1] He later met a local Satanist who told him "You don't ever have to feel guilty about anything. The only law is that you are true to your inner self. If you want to kill somebody, that's okay. What's bad to them is good for us. Get it?"[1]

On April 18, 1984, nine-year-old Mei Leung was tragically found murdered, having been physically assaulted, raped, and stabbed to death before her body was hung from a pipe in the basement of her apartment building.[5] This heinous act marked the beginning of the young man's violent spree, though it remained unidentified at the time. Two months later, on June 28, 1984, he targeted 79-year-old Jennie Vincow in a burglary that turned deadly. After researching the area and finding the people there to be flush with cash, the young man chose the house of 79-year-old Jennie Vincow to burglarize and therefore continue his access to the increasingly expensive drugs he'd grown accustomed to. Unfortunately for both him and Jennie, his victim was home and discovered him before he was able to escape. No one knows exactly what happened after that moment, but Jennie's son Jack came home later to find "a window screen missing, the front door unlocked and his mother's belongings scattered around the home."[4] He then found what no son ever wants to find - his mother lying on the floor with stab wounds all over and her throat slashed. The medical examiner later found that in addition to stabbing and killing Ms. Vincow, the young man had also raped her before nearly decapitating her.

This was it. There was no going back.

CHAPTER 13

On August 31, 1985, the infamous "Nightstalker" finally had a name: Richard Ramirez. His year-long killing spree came to an end after killing at least 14 people in and around Los Angeles, California. As investigators dug deeper, the timeline of his violence turned out to be even darker than anyone realized.

During the investigation, it was revealed that Ramirez had committed his first murder in April of 1984, a fact confirmed only in 2009, over 20 years later.[2] His brutal assault on Mei Leung marked the beginning of a series of horrific crimes. Following that, he murdered Jennie Vincow, the first victim he would later be convicted of killing in 1985. From that point on, his brutality escalated further, leaving a trail of victims across Southern California who had the misfortune of crossing his path.

Following these two gruesome murders, Ramirez killed Dayle Okazaki, Tsai Lian Yu, Vincent Zazzara, Maxine Zazzara, William Doi, Mabel Bell, Mary Louise Cannon, Joyce Lucille Nelson, Maxon Kneiding, Lela Kneiding, Chainarong Khovananth, and Elyas Abowath– individuals who deserve to be more famous than their killer. These men and women were blameless besides being in the wrong place at the wrong time and their inability to predict their final breath. They were raped, beaten, and shot. They were mutilated and forced to swear to Satan. They were bludgeoned with tire irons, stomped on, and abducted.[2] Even Ramirez himself later acknowledged how impossible it is for ordinary people to comprehend, much less defend against, that level of predatory intent.

When asked how society can protect itself from serial killers, Ramirez said there is "no protection against a mass murderer" and that a serial killer takes advantage of "opportunities" and "being in the right place at the right time." He added that people can try to protect themselves by "taking precautions, locking your doors, having your keys ready when you open doors … being on guard," but that normal people "do not think like a serial killer" and have "no conception of what is going on in a killer's mind."[1]

Richard Ramirez was convicted in 1989 but before his sentencing, he was asked if he had any final remarks. His response was as follows:

"I don't know even why I'm wasting my breath, but what the hell. For so what is said of my life, there have been lies in the past and there will be lies in the future. I don't believe in the hypocritical, moralistic dogma of this so-called civilized society. I need not look beyond this room to see all the liars, the haters, the killers, the crooks, the paranoid cowards. Truly the trematodes of the earth, each one of his own legal profession. You maggots, hypocrites one and all. We are all expendable for a cause. No one knows that better than those who kill for policy, clandestinely or openly as to the governments of the world which kill in the name of God and country and for whatever else they deem appropriate. I don't need to hear all of society's rationalizations. I've heard them before, and the fact remains that what is, is. You don't understand me. You are not expected to. You are not capable of it. I am beyond your experience. I am beyond good and evil. Legions of the night, nightbreed, repeat not the errors of night prowler and show no mercy. I will be avenged. Lucifer dwells in us all. That's it."[4]

After being sentenced to death, he rolled his eyes and responded, "Big deal. Death always went with the territory. See you in Disneyland."[3]

CHAPTER 14

Ramirez's life began as no child's life should, and to no fault of his own. Between the abusive father and the cousin who had far too much influence on him, he was set up for failure even before the temporal-lobe epilepsy diagnosis came into play. When asked in an interview why he thinks serial killers are more prevalent these days, Ramirez himself responded that "I believe that… tension in the workplace and also lack of jobs, and the way families are brought up, and child abuse, it's like a recipe. Drugs, poverty, child abuse– all this creates angry individuals."[1] It goes without saying that his childhood was a key factor in how he grew up, but he was also the only known serial killer among his siblings, so what is it about his recipe, to use his words, that created the man we know as Richard Ramirez?

While there is no definitive information anywhere about exactly what Ramirez's psychological pathology was, there is evidence that he scored 31 out of 40 on the Hare Psychopathy Checklist, which indicates a high level of psychopathic traits. A score this high is generally followed by a diagnosis of Anti-Social Personality Disorder but could indicate that he was a psychopath or a sociopath. Both these terms are used interchangeably by the general public but mean slightly different things. Psychopaths tend to be cold, calculated, and emotionally cut off from the world around them. They usually show little empathy, remorse, or guilt, and their antisocial behavior is often planned and controlled. They can blend in easily because they know how to mimic charm and stability even when nothing about their internal world matches that. Sociopaths, on the other hand, are more shaped by their environment. Trauma, neglect, or chaotic upbringing usually play a major role in how they develop. They tend to be impulsive, emotionally reactive, and inconsistent with their behavior. A sociopath may feel flashes of guilt or attachment, but it never lasts long enough to guide their choices. Their wrongdoing is more chaotic and unpredictable and usually driven by emotion rather than strategy.[3]

Based on this information, it seems more likely that Ramirez was a sociopath than a psychopath. He did have a conscious, and while that conscious was initially burdened by the discrepancy between his Christian upbringing and his "evil" thoughts and desires, he did finally give in and succumb to his newfound satanic beliefs. Additionally, his violence and instability were built over time through trauma, brain injuries, abuse, and the influence of his cousin. While psychopaths are generally emotionally detached from the beginning, sociopaths are usually shaped by their environment, and his environment was a disaster from every angle. His behavior was also way too chaotic for a typical psychopath. Psychopaths plan, control, and calculate, but not Ramirez. His crimes were messy and impulsive. He left victims alive, failed to erase the evidence, switched weapons, changed his patterns constantly, and acted out of whatever urge hit him at the moment.

The biggest difference between Ramirez and a typical psychopathic personality, though, may have been his attachment to his cousin. While no one knows exactly what he was thinking or feeling at any given time, it is pretty clear that he was attached to and heavily influenced by Mike.

This is more consistent with sociopathic behavior because the relationship almost felt desperate. Ramirez clung to his cousin, absorbed his worldviews, and purportedly tried to make him proud with everything he did. Put simply, a psychopath just wouldn't care about any of this.

Ramirez also demonstrated narcissistic personality disorder, primarily based on how much he seemed to enjoy being known as the Nightstalker. Calling people "narcissists" has become more and more popular in the 21st century, but that term is thrown around without a true understanding of what it means. The DSM-5 (Diagnostic and Statistical Manual of Mental Disorders) qualifies a narcissist as generally putting one's own needs before the needs of others, and more specifically exhibiting the following characteristics:[4]

- Grandiose sense of self-importance
- Belief in superiority
- Entitlement
- Lack of empathy
- Frequent fantasies about having or deserving
- Need for admiration
- Willingness to exploit others
- Frequent envy

Someone with these traits might look confident on the surface, but most of their behavior is really about protecting themselves from feeling exposed or inadequate. It can show up as perfectionism, withdrawal, anger when criticized, or avoiding anything that risks failure, all in an effort to keep their fragile sense of self from cracking.

Ramirez showed a lot of patterns that line up with narcissism, mostly through how desperate he was to feel powerful and superior. He built an entire identity around domination, control, and being feared, which is exactly what someone does when they need external validation to hold themselves together. His obsession with being seen as special or chosen, along with how enraged he became when he felt challenged or dismissed, fits the kind of fragile self-esteem you see in narcissistic personality traits.

Finally, Ramirez's acts of sexual abuse and rape and eventually murder line up with sexual sadism, a paraphilic disorder that is characterized by gaining pleasure from the pain of others. Research from crime scene analyses shows that while sexual sadism isn't synonymous with rape, it often involves a mix of forced sexual acts and domination that can escalate into rape or even murder. Although it appears in fewer than ten percent of rapists, it shows up far more often among those who commit sexual homicides, with rates reported around one third.[5] Starting when he was a teenager, Ramirez had fantasies about "taking" women for himself, enjoying the thought of dominating them and feeling the power and control that would come with that. His sexually sadistic tendencies moved fairly quickly from dreaming about it to acting, and he soon found himself in the company of other sexual sadists such as Ted Bundy and John Wayne Gacy.

When we step back and look at the bigger picture, we have to acknowledge the limits of what anyone can truly know about his mind. Almost everything we have about Richard Ramirez comes from interviews, media coverage, and retrospective speculation, not a full psychiatric workup, so there are real gaps in the story. That uncertainty doesn't soften what he did. It just highlights how layers of trauma, possible neurological problems, warped belief systems, and deep personality pathology stacked on top of each other until he became the person the world now knows as the Nightstalker. And with that psychological groundwork already in place, the shift from petty theft to his first brutal act of violence became a straight line rather than a leap.

PART 4

HUNTING FOR A HUSBAND

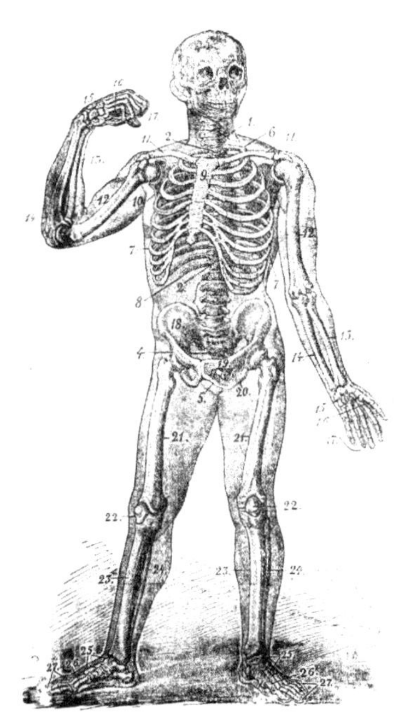

CHAPTER 15

It's the mid-1800s in Norway and the young girl has been laboring on her family's farm for hours already, including but not limited to tilling the earth, planting and weeding, harvesting, milking the cows and caring for the animals, cooking and cleaning, and other various home and farm tasks. She's going through the motions but all she can think is how one day she'll escape this way of life. By whatever means necessary, she will marry a rich man and propel her life forward in the way it was always supposed to go.

But for now, she's impoverished in Norway with no way to get out.

Born on November 11, 1859, the girl was the youngest of eight children. While very little is known about her early life, what is known is that her family was one of the poorest in their community of Inngbya.[1] Her father was born in the district and leased a small amount of a local farm, where he owned two cows, three sheep, and one goat,[2] as well as enough crops to keep his family from starving. In the winter, he supplemented his work as a farmer by working as a stonemason, shaping, cutting, and installing stone to build or repair structures such as buildings and bridges.[1]

As was common with children of poor families, the girl was expected to labor on the farm and in the home from a young age. As she got a little older, her primary responsibility became fetching the family's daily ration of Snurkvist, twigs used for kindling that the family required due to their inability to afford wood for their fire. The kids in her community knew this about her and began calling her "Snurkvistpala," which translates roughly as "Paul's twig-daughter."[1]

The teenager was confirmed at the Evangelical Lutheran Church in 1874 at age 14. Her religious instructor said she was "good in religious knowledge and diligence," a compliment that was not freely given out. This description of the teenager was typical. She was known as a hard worker, well-behaved, diligent, and clever.[1] Interestingly, unlike her serial killing counterparts, there is no evidence of drug abuse, childhood trauma, or family members with mental illnesses. This doesn't necessarily mean none of that happened, as there is very little information about her upbringing at all, but it does seem as though there would be information out there about her childhood if any of that was true.

The teenager's parents weren't alone in their struggles to provide basic needs for their family. Norway in the late 1800s was packed with working families who watched the country grow richer while their own wages barely moved. Most lived on small plots of land or took whatever labor they could get, and even then the pay was so low that saving for a better life was almost impossible. With too many people chasing too few jobs, poverty became a trap that entire communities couldn't escape. It made leaving for America feel less like a dream and more like the only real way out,[4] and a third of Norway's population did just that between 1860 and 1910, with about 800,000 people emigrating in total from 1882 into the 1920s.[3]

Long term poverty in childhood has been linked to higher rates of both internalizing problems, like anxiety and chronic stress, and externalizing problems, like aggression or difficulty regulating behavior.[6,7] Children who grow below the poverty line show increasing behavior problems over time and measurable differences in brain regions tied to emotion regulation and decision making. Additionally, kids who spend their early years in economic hardship tend to develop more stress, more emotional withdrawal, and more outward behavioral issues as they grow. Another interesting study found that, while poverty itself doesn't necessarily cause behavioral issues, hardships surrounding poverty such as parental strain and inconsistent caregiving can correlate with child behavior problems.[5] These patterns don't mean poverty causes mental illness or criminal behavior, but they do show that growing up under chronic strain makes certain struggles more likely.

The stress of poverty often forces parents to work long hours or multiple jobs, which can leave children on their own more than anyone would prefer. When caregivers are stretched thin just to afford food or basic needs, supervision becomes inconsistent and kids end up raising themselves. That lack of structure or emotional support can compound the stress already present in low-income households. It creates an environment where kids have to figure out survival, problem solving, and boundaries without steady guidance.[5]

None of this gives us a clear explanation of what shaped our young antagonist. We don't have records about what her daily life looked like or how her family handled the pressures of poverty. However, it's in our human nature to want to look back and figure out the "why" behind behaviors we can't understand, and the research that shows these correlations can give us a good starting point. Thankfully, history clears up quite a bit more when it comes to the teenager's adolescence, so there's about to be a lot less guessing and a lot more facts.

CHAPTER 16

She was 17 years old, tall, had the most captivating blue eyes, and finally thought that she had found her way out of poverty. The teenager had been seeing the son of a local wealthy family that would be her ticket to a better life if everything went as she planned. As things happen at that age, she had recently found herself pregnant and decided to tell her lover at their high school dance. Despite the fact that he explicitly told her never to approach him in public and regularly told her his family would never accept her, she was sure he would be ecstatic- or at least do the right thing- when he found out about his baby.

To no one's surprise but the teenager, things did not go as planned. The boy was quiet immediately after hearing the girl was pregnant, and then began vehemently insisting that the child was not his. After all, he knew many who would attest that the teenager regularly lifted her skirts for anyone that moved, breathed, and had the right parts. When she started to argue with him and he saw that she wasn't going to back down, he swung his fist into her stomach while calling her a whore and kept on swinging until she was on the ground, then continued the abuse by kicking her with the heel of his shoe.

Before long, the teenager felt the blood flowing and knew that with it, her child was dying. Walking or crawling, she somehow made it home and crawled into bed before anyone knew she had ever left, but she was permanently changed. She decided to tell no one and to put the incident behind her, but she swore she would never show weakness again.[1]

Historical accounts don't line up perfectly here, but the story goes that not long after this traumatic event, the teenage boy was diagnosed with stomach cancer and died soon after. At the time, ugly rumors started circulating that it wasn't cancer at all but poison… and that the teenager was responsible.[1] Whether that's the truth or a tale people crafted later, once her crimes came to light, is something we'll never be able to pin down. Still, the accusation lines up uncomfortably well with what she would go on to do

Soon after the death of her unborn child and the child's teenage father, the young woman decided to follow in the footsteps of the hundreds of thousands of Norwegians who had found their way to America. Her older sister had emigrated years earlier and invited the young woman to move in with her and her new husband in Chicago, Illinois. While the journey to America wasn't pleasant, it ended soon enough and the young woman found herself in her new home with a new Americanized name and a job working as a housekeeper.[2]

In Chicago, the young woman was surrounded by riches she had never even dreamt of. Everywhere she looked she saw expensive jewelry and clothing and so, so much money. Even her sister was living a comfortable life, with a nice house, five children who loved her, a husband who worked hard for their money, and her own housekeeper. The young woman felt pangs of resentment but knew she had to continue working hard so she could eventually buy her way out or, more appealingly, marry a rich man and have lots of babies.

When asked later on, her sister said the young woman "never seemed to care for a man for his own self, only for the money or luxury he was able to give her."[2] From the time she was young, her dream was to marry rich so she could live the life she felt she deserved– not one of laboring from dawn until dusk, barely making ends meet, and being teased mercilessly. In the young woman's eyes, she should be the one hiring people for the labor and using her words and actions to make people feel however she deemed necessary.

In her work as a housemaid, she discovered that she could feel some of that power by sleeping with the husbands of the women who hired her to clean their homes. She enjoyed the looks she got from the men when they laid eyes on her while cleaning, but what she enjoyed even more was the money and gifts she received from them. She felt a certain superiority when the female homeowners would criticize her for this or that, all the while knowing their husbands wanted her more than they wanted their wives, and she could ruin their lives with that knowledge.[1]

The young woman finally met and married her knight in shining armor in 1884, when she was 24 years old and he was 29 years old. Her new husband spoiled her with a great place to live, beautiful jewels, clothes she'd always hungered for, and anything else she asked for. Having realized the first part of her dream, though, she now hungered for part two: children. She knew that she wouldn't truly be satisfied until her whole dream was fulfilled. By all accounts, the young woman was great with kids. She was very involved with the Sunday School programs at her church and there wasn't a child who didn't love her. She also volunteered with homeless and orphaned children– anything to be able to use her maternal gifts.[2] Unfortunately, no matter how hard the young woman tried, she was unable to get pregnant.

Despite having married a man who was crazy about her, the young woman continued her affairs with the husbands of the women who maintained her employment. Why would she stop if it was still getting her closer to where she thought she should be? Her resentment and jealousy toward her sister also continued to grow, as she didn't understand why her sister should get the wealthy husband *and* the house full of children. Her sister frequently complained about how hard it was to have five kids, so the young woman decided to help her sister out… she would adopt her sister's youngest daughter. Her sister immediately said "no," shocked that the young woman would even consider that as an appropriate suggestion. Not only was it an absurd request, but she also remembered the last time her youngest had stayed with the young woman; despite members of the church fawning over how good she was with kids, the child had been uneasy the whole time and begged her parents to pick her up early. The young woman was furious when she was told "No." Her sister could always have more kids, but this may be her only chance for a child![1] The sisters' relationship quickly unraveled from here, as the young woman rarely visited or even spoke to her sister after that.

In 1890, the young woman finally got her chance. A neighbor and close friend of the young woman and her husband was dying and would leave her children without a mother. After spending days doting on the mother, she begged her to let her raise the youngest daughter. After making her swear she would raise the child as her own, the mother accepted the girl's request and gave up her youngest daughter.

The young woman was overjoyed with her new daughter, and over time her home would grow to welcome as many as 10-12 children at a time, whether from overcrowded orphanages or parents needing respite. This also became a way for the young woman to get closer to her dream of wealth, as she was usually played handsomely to adopt these unwanted children.[1] The young woman loved these children at first, but the needier they got, the less interested she became. Soon after their births, two of the children died of acute inflammation of the bowels and hydrocephalus.[2] However, because infant death was so common, neither of these deaths were looked into like they probably should have been if the medical examiners had known who their adoptive mother truly was.

CHAPTER 17

After a while, the woman decided the money her family was making from her husband's job, her affairs, and their foster children wasn't enough. Having a head for business, she convinced her husband to buy a small building, and the two opened a confectionery store selling sweets, cigarettes, newspapers, and basic grocery items.[1] The store struggled almost immediately. It never attracted steady customers, and whatever profit it did make was short-lived. Still, what happened next proved far more lucrative than the business itself. Less than a year after opening, a kerosene lamp supposedly exploded, starting a fire that burned the store to the ground. Though there were whispers of arson[2], the woman and her husband received a sizable insurance payout, enough to relocate to a wealthier neighborhood in Chicago.[1] Misfortune had worked in their favor.

Between 1896 and 1898, the couple had four more children. It remains unclear whether the children were adopted or born to them, but two died under suspicious circumstances not long after arriving in the household, and once again the couple collected insurance payouts. Two years later, on April 10, 1900, another fire broke out, destroying $650 worth of household goods that were conveniently insured. Less than a week later, her husband fell ill, complaining of a severe headache. The woman insisted he take a medication she provided, and after lying down to rest, he never woke up. Neighbors later reported hearing him cry out, "You poisoned me!" and the first doctor to examine the body immediately suspected strychnine poisoning.[1] The woman claimed a pharmacist had mistakenly given her strychnine instead of quinine, but with no proof and an autopsy denied, his death was officially ruled the result of a sudden cerebral hemorrhage.[2]

The timing was almost too perfect. The fire did not merely precede the death of the woman's husband, it set the stage for a rare overlap in his two life insurance policies, ensuring the maximum payout. Adjusted for inflation, the $2,000 and $3,000 life insurance policies, along with the insured property losses, would total well over $200,000 today. For a working family at the turn of the century, it was an extraordinary sum, and yet another moment where tragedy and financial gain collided in deeply unsettling ways.[2]

Shortly after her husband's death, the woman moved to La Porte, Indiana, purchasing a large farm and starting over once again. Not long after settling in, word reached her that a certain handsome man she and her husband once knew had recently been widowed. The woman was no beauty herself, having been described as a "fat, heavy-featured woman with a big head covered with a mop of mud-colored hair, small eyes, supported by feet grotesquely small."[3] Her property, however, at over 40 acres, more than made up for her lack in the looks department. She had little trouble attracting men, not least of all this recent widower.[2]

On April 2, 1902, almost exactly two years after her first husband's mysterious death, the new couple was married. Five days later, her husband's seven-month-old daughter died a sudden and tragic death. While the doctor believed the child had been smothered by her stepmother, who had been alone with her at the time, there was no proof, and the official cause of death was listed as edema of the lungs[1].

Eight months later, on December 16, 1902, the woman's husband died as well, supposedly after a meat grinder fell from a high shelf and crushed his skull while he bent down to retrieve his shoes. The explanation was unusual but not impossible, and authorities initially prepared to accept it as a tragic accident.[2]

Doubts surfaced almost immediately. Neighbors noted the woman's calm demeanor, the oddly staged scene, and inconsistencies in her account of events. An inquest was convened, during which the coroner's jury heard testimony about the placement of the grinder, the force required to cause such injuries, and the woman's shifting timeline. Despite widespread suspicion, the jury ultimately ruled the death accidental, citing insufficient evidence to prove otherwise. The case was closed legally, but not socially. In the court of public opinion, whispers followed the woman wherever she went, marking the first real fracture between her and the community.[2]

The death of her second husband seemed to be the final straw. The girl found herself increasingly isolated, watched closely, and quietly avoided. She frequently got into spats with her neighbors, letting her animals roam onto their land and paying to retrieve them, then taking her revenge by forcing their animals onto her land and making them pay to get them back. Whatever charm she once had no longer worked in her favor, and La Porte began to see her less as a widow deserving sympathy and more as a woman surrounded by too much death.

It was the winter of 1904 when the woman discovered the power of personal advertisements. She published the following notice in her local paper:

> *Personal — Comely widow who owns a large farm in one of the finest districts of La Porte County, Indiana,*

desires to make the acquaintance of gentleman equally well provided, with view of joining fortunes. No replies by letter considered unless sender is willing to follow answer with personal visit. Triflers need not apply.[1]

The first man to answer the ad was a man in his thirties named Olaf. The two got along well, and Olaf quickly became comfortable on the farm, earning the affection of both the woman's children and her neighbors. Encouraged by her kindness and her frequent invitations to her bedroom, Olaf grew confident that the relationship was headed toward marriage, even telling his parents he expected to wed soon.[1] But over time, the woman's attitude toward him changed. She became jealous of his closeness with her children and distant in her affections. Not long after, Olaf vanished. When friends and family asked where he had gone, the woman curtly replied that he had abandoned his duties in the middle of the season, leaving her without a farmhand.

It was a small disappearance, easily explained away, and yet it marked something new. For the first time, a man entered the woman's life without leaving any record of where he went next. What had once been a pattern of misfortune was quietly becoming something else entirely.

CHAPTER 18

Belle Gunness lived and died over a century ago. Because of that, factual information on her is difficult to find and the various books and research out there seems to contradict each other at every turn. However, while there is plenty of doubt about who she killed and how she did it, there is no doubt that she did, indeed, kill.

Following the sudden disappearance of Olaf Lindboe from Belle's farm, Henry Gurholt was hired as a farmhand and immediately took a liking to it. In a letter he wrote to his mother shortly after arriving, he said "I am being treated almost the same as one of the family."[2] Unfortunately, he may have been treated a little too similarly to her family, as he, too, disappeared one day in August 1905. Numerous human remains were discovered on Belle's farm later on, but neither Lindboe nor Gurholt's bodies were ever definitively identified. However, due to the timing and circumstances surrounding the disappearances of the men, and the fact that they were never heard from again, both men were presumed victims of Belle Gunness.

Despite the disappearances, men continued responding to Belle's newest ad:

- *WANTED — A woman who owns a beautifully located a valuable farm in first class condition, wants a good and reliable man as partner in*

The postman later reported that she received anywhere from one to ten letters a day, presumably from suitors hoping to woo the wealthy woman with all the land. Among the men who sold all of their belongings and brought with them anywhere from $1000 to $2000 in cash ($40,000 to $50,000 in today's dollars) were George Berry from Illinois, Christian Hilkven from Wisconsin, Emil Tell from Kansas, Ole Budsberg from Wisconsin, John Moe from Minnesota, and many more. Witnesses say a different man came to stay with her nearly every week, and left soon after without anyone seeing their departure and, stranger still, without their suitcases or trunks.[2]

Of these, only Ole Budsberg's body was discovered.[3] The rest simply vanished but were treated by historians (if not the local justice system) as likely victims of Belle Gunness.

By the Fall of 1906, Belle's 16-year-old foster daughter Jennie (the child Belle had adopted from her dying friend years ago) had grown into a beautiful girl with plenty of men who fawned over her. Her closest friend and confidant was Emil Greening, another young farmhand of Belle's[2]. From what Emil said later, talking to him had made Jennie realize she had been manipulated by Belle and gaslit into rejecting her biological father, who had tried to take Jennie back once he was in a sound emotional and financial position.[1] She was afraid of Belle and did whatever she could to placate her every chance she could. According to another acquaintance of Jennie's, Jess Dickinson, Belle was seen brutally beating Jennie on occasion; through tears of fear and anger, Jennie showed Jess the bruises and marks from the beatings and Jess was appalled but not surprised.[1]

Over time, Jennie became more and more rebellious, assertive, and angry toward Belle. She stopped trying to appease her foster mother and began to openly argue with her and let her anger show. Around this time, in the winter of 1906, Belle decided to send Jennie to college in Los Angeles. With an understanding of how frustrated Jennie was with her foster-mother, it can be assumed that she was delighted at the thought of leaving Belle and starting over. Her suitors were obviously disappointed and wanted to tell her goodbye, but when they came to see her off, Belle told them she had already left. Despite sending several letters over the next year, Jennie's friends and suitors never heard from her again.[1,2]

In April of 1908, Jennie's body was found on Belle's farm. The local newspaper at the time wrote this:

> *"This adopted daughter was a simple-minded, quiet girl, who was known to the neighbors chiefly because she did more work than any hired man. She was Belle Gunness' pretty slave. And yet the mistress feared the slave. So the slave died, and was buried in quicklime in the same death garden that had received the bodies of others who died because they had money."*[3]

By 1907, Belle Gunness had refined her system. That year, she hired Ray Lamphere as a farmhand, a rarely sober drifter with a volatile temperament and an obvious devotion to her. Before long, Lamphere became more than just hired help. The two entered into a sexual relationship, one that gave Lamphere the impression he held a special place in Belle's life. He worked her farm, defended her reputation, and obeyed her demands, convinced he was indispensable to her.

But Lamphere was never the man Belle was truly investing in. As early as 1906, Belle had begun a correspondence with

Andrew Helgelien, a Norwegian immigrant living in South Dakota. Over the next eighteen months, Belle sent him between seventy-five and eighty letters. While Helgelien's replies were lost, Belle's letters survived, offering a rare and chilling window into her manipulation. She flattered him relentlessly, presenting herself as both discerning and devoted. In one letter she wrote:

> *"Dear friend, you impress me with being a good man with a strong and honest character. A real genuine Norwegian in every respect, and it is difficult to find such a man and not every woman appreciates. There are plenty of these American 'dudes' around here but I would not even look at them, no matter how often they asked me."*[2]

Belle crafted an idyllic version of her life in La Porte, portraying herself as a hardworking widow with a prosperous farm and limitless potential. She told Helgelien he would have far greater opportunities there than where he was, assuring him that his capital would grow faster under her guidance. Her language grew increasingly intimate and exaggerated. "I do not think a queen could be good enough for you,"[2] she wrote. "We shall be so happy when you once get here."[2] She urged him to sell everything he owned and come at once, insisting he tell no one of his plans because she wanted to "surprise" his family. In January 1908, Andrew Helgelien finally arrived in La Porte.

Lamphere had no idea the correspondence existed. The shock was immediate and humiliating. Belle informed him that Helgelien would be taking over his bedroom and that Lamphere could sleep in the barn. According to Lamphere, the relationship between himself and Belle changed overnight. As recently as the night before Helgelien's arrival,

Belle had still been visiting Lamphere's room. Now, she no longer had use for him.

On January 6, Belle accompanied Helgelien to the bank so he could redeem three certificates of deposit. The banker explained the process would take four or five days. When the pair returned on January 14, the banker suggested issuing a cashier's check, a safer option given the large sum involved. Belle refused and demanded the money in cash, an amount equivalent to roughly $75,000 today.[2]

That night, Belle sent Lamphere away on an errand that would keep him gone until morning. The next time Andrew Helgelien was seen was in April 1908 when his remains were discovered on Belle Gunness' land.

On April 28th, the Gunness farm burnt to the ground until there was nothing but bricks left. The bodies of Belle and her children were discovered among the burnt rubble. Strangely, though, Belle's head was missing and her body was significantly smaller than anyone remembered it being when she was alive.

At first it was assumed that Ray Lamphere, out of anger and heartbreak, had committed arson and burnt down the farm. After all, just days prior Belle had been spreading news of her "fear" of Ray because he had threatened to burn down the farm.[2] However, days later after discovering dozens of bodies and body parts strewn about beneath the farm, the community's suspicion and hatred turned to Belle, assuming she had committed murder and arson.. And had possibly faked her own death as well.[4]

As with all of Belle's story, it will never be known what really happened on that fateful La Porte farm over 100 years ago. Belle Gunness either died or escaped before being tried for her numerous crimes. Had she been held accountable for the murders, she surely would have been found guilty of the deaths of at least the 12 bodies found on her farm, if not more.[5] At the end of the day, no one will ever know exactly how many deaths were caused by the Murderess of La Porte, Indiana.

CHAPTER 19

When you hear the term "serial killer," what gender do you immediately picture? If you're like most Americans, it's probably a man, despite the fact that women are also capable of murder. Interestingly, as of 2023, women accounted for approximately 8% of all serial murders. According to Jana Monroe, one of the first female FBI agents, the reason women are less likely to commit serial murder than men is that "Men tend to express aggression outwardly, while women are more likely to internalize aggression, leading to self-harm, depression, or relational manipulation rather than physical violence."[1] Penn State psychologist Marissa Harrison says this, "Men kill overtly; they leave more brutal evidence behind. Female serial killers kill covertly and use means that are not as readily detectible. Police won't likely know it's homicide until they string together a series of deaths that are statistically unlikely—a hospital setting, numerous dead spouses, many dead children."[1]

Interestingly, while it is generally assumed that women kill due to broken hearts, revenge, or power, 98% of female serial killers kill for financial gain[2]. This is largely in line with Belle Gunness, who, while it is unknown exactly when she started killing, definitively killed for financial gain. After receiving the insurance payout for her dead children and husband, she likely realized how much faster her lifelong dream of wealth would come to fruition if she climbed on the backs of others.

Female serial killers are far more methodical and calculated than most people realize. Research shows that women who commit multiple murders often operate in roles where they are trusted such as caretakers, mothers, nurses, or spouses. They exploit that trust, using it to disguise their crimes, which are often carried out quietly and without the spectacle that male killers tend to leave behind. Poison is the most common weapon, but suffocation, smothering, and other methods that mimic natural causes are also frequent. Unlike male killers, who often target strangers, female serial killers overwhelmingly choose victims they know such as family members, spouses, or people under their care. In fact, children, the elderly, and the sick make up the majority of their victims, simply because these targets are more vulnerable and less able to resist.[2]

Most female serial killers are not social outcasts. Many, like Belle Gunness, are married at least once and about half have children. Average or above-average attractiveness is also common, a trait they can use to manipulate those around them. Childhood trauma, abuse, or parental neglect is overrepresented among these women, suggesting early life stressors may contribute to the development of these behaviors, though nothing is definitive.[2] Substance abuse and mental health issues, such as depression, sociopathy, or Munchausen by proxy, appear more often than in the general population, but again, these are patterns rather than guarantees.

In short, female serial killers are far from the archetypal image of the vengeful or lovesick woman. They are strategic, often financially or materially motivated, and they exploit societal assumptions about women to mask their crimes. For Belle Gunness, her focus on financial gain, her ability to cultivate trust, and her cold manipulation of family and spouses fit the profile precisely. She was not an anomaly; she was an extreme, real-world example of a pattern that psychology and criminology studies have been trying to understand for decades.

PART 5

A SIN WORSE THAN RAPE

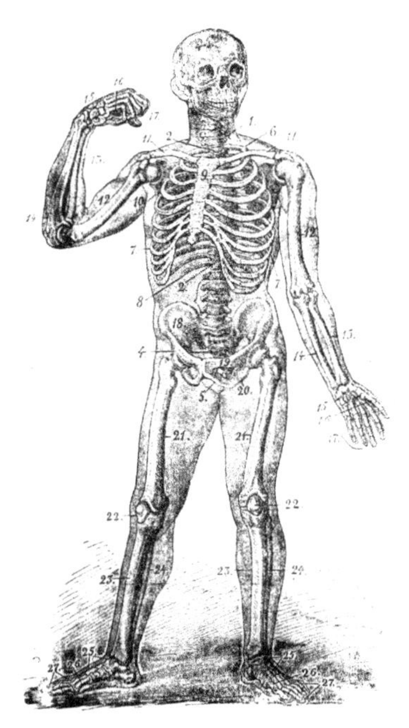

CHAPTER 20

It's a dreary, rainy day in Washington State but inside feels no warmer or safer than outside. The 12-year-old boy has just awoken, yet again, to a wet bed after having yet another nightmare. He starts softly crying, not because he's embarrassed, but because he knows what's coming before it even happens. Soon enough, his fear is realized as his mother puts him in the shower, partially undresses herself, and scrubs his genitals until they're clean but raw. The feelings he is experiencing has him confused, frustrated, and angry when, later on, he hears his mother making fun of him to his brothers. He stays upstairs for a while longer, waiting for the shame to dissipate and the family to forget what had happened… again.

The second of three boys, the boy was born on February 18, 1949 in Salt Lake City, Utah. His father was a bus driver, his mother a salesclerk. They had a good life and lived in nice houses, although they were constantly moving around so it was difficult for the boy to make friends. He also had dyslexia and had trouble reading words, which was frustrating for him when it seemed like everyone else could read just fine. Another point of shame for him was his incessant bedwetting. When he was little it didn't seem like that big of a deal because everyone else was doing it too, but it became more of a problem when he couldn't seem to stop even into junior high.[1]

Bedwetting is not just a bathroom issue. It is often connected to emotional, behavioral, and social problems, which can make life harder for kids and more stressful for parents. Research[2] shows that many children who struggle with bedwetting also have mental health or behavioral conditions. In some studies, nearly 9 out of 10 children with enuresis had at least one additional psychiatric diagnosis.

The most common issues linked to bedwetting are behavior problems and emotional struggles. These include ADHD, conduct disorder, anxiety, oppositional defiant disorder, obsessive-compulsive symptoms, and tic disorders. Kids with bedwetting are especially likely to show externalizing behaviors like impulsivity, defiance, and aggression. This connection does not disappear as kids get older. Studies of adolescents show that bedwetting is still linked to higher rates of anxiety, social withdrawal, ADHD symptoms, conduct problems, and even suicidal behavior.

In the boy's case, his bedwetting was shameful not only because no one else his age was still doing it, but also because of what came after and how it changed the direction of his entire life. But we'll come back to that shortly.

In addition to the boy's dyslexia and bedwetting, he had seasonal allergies and always seemed to need a tissue or t-shirt sleeve or blanket to wipe his nose on. By themselves, none of these things were too cumbersome, but put together they made him feel like he couldn't do anything right, and his mom made it clear that he made far too much work for her.

School was tough for the boy. His brothers were favored over him by his parents and, seemingly, the general public. His dyslexia and low IQ ensured that he stayed behind in school and never felt on sure footing with academics. His struggles at school were not just about effort or motivation.

Intelligence testing placed the boy well below average, and that label followed him everywhere. Teachers adjusted their expectations downward. Peers noticed he was slower, easier to confuse, and easier to mock. Research[3] has consistently shown that children with lower IQ scores are at greater risk for academic failure, social rejection, and chronic stress, all of which compound over time rather than resolve on their own. For this boy, school became less a place of learning and more a daily reminder that he did not measure up.

Low cognitive ability in childhood has also been linked to increased vulnerability to later psychological problems, particularly when paired with adverse home environments. Children with lower IQs are less equipped to navigate conflict, interpret social cues accurately, or escape harmful situations, making them more susceptible to anxiety, depression, and externalizing behaviors as they age.[3] In a household where patience was thin and affection felt conditional, these limitations mattered. The boy did not have the tools to push back, to advocate for himself, or to imagine a future where things might look different. Instead, frustration settled inward, quietly, laying groundwork that would not fully reveal itself until much later.

Not only did he have a difficult time with academics, but his skills in the relational department were lacking as well. The boy was small and therefore easy to pick on. One of the kids he went to school with was named Dennis and he would regularly wait for the boy in an alley by the school and beat him up, leaving him bloodied and bruised for his walk back home. When he got home, his father would get angry with him for having blood on his clothes and for getting beat up, even telling him once, "if you come home one more time beat up I'll beat your ass myself.[1]" After this, though, the boy's father taught him how to stand up for himself and fight. Later, he said, "I got Dennis down on the ground once and held his arms."[1]

Despite learning how to stand up for himself, he still found himself angry for the majority of the time. He started imagining who he could hurt and how he would do it. He became an even better fighter and started winning fights once he learned how to pin his opponents by putting his feet or knees on their shoulders. Around 8-years-old he started setting fires to garages and outbuildings, enjoying not only the look and feel of the flame but also the chaos that ensued after the fire was started. Taken together, the fire setting and chronic bedwetting place the boy squarely within what later researchers would label the Macdonald Triad, a controversial but often-cited framework used to describe troubling patterns in childhood behavior. It doesn't predict who will become violent, but it does show that by a very young age, his anger, fixation, and need for control were already taking shape.

Later, the boy also admitted to stalking girls starting in elementary school and into middle school. "…I'd have a…a hard on and… think of the woman as a goal and be on the opposite side of the street. And find out where she lived…"[4] He didn't admit to going any further than stalking until he was a little older, but the stage was set and clearly the intentions were there. By the time he reached adolescence, the boy was no longer just fantasizing about violence, he was rehearsing it, and the line between thought and action was already thinning.

CHAPTER 21

The older the young boy grew, the harder things got for him. His relationship with his mother was especially peculiar, as he seemed to both fear her and feel attraction toward her, which was about as confusing as things could get for a boy of his age. However, due to the nature of his bedwetting, his mother continued treating him as though he was a toddler, cleaning his genitals herself even as he was making his way through elementary and middle school. Later in life, the boy told his psychologist that all these years later he still had vivid memories of his mother washing his genitals after he wet the bed.[1]

Not only would this have been humiliating, but also highly arousing for an adolescent boy. As a teenager and beyond, he fantasized about killing her because of how sexually attracted he was to her and the way it made him think and feel about her. This kind of displaced matricide is common among serial murderers. It reflects a desire to kill the original object of sexual fixation, in this case his mother, but instead acting out that violence on others, repeating the same symbolic murder again and again[1]. The teenager told the psychologist later that he "thought about stabbing her in the chest or in the heart maybe uh. . . . um. . . . maybe uh . . . cut her face and chest."[1]

One theory often used to understand thoughts, feelings, and eventually behaviors like this is displaced matricide, the idea that violent urges originally directed toward the mother are later redirected onto other victims. The principle behind this is that the mother becomes the first object of intense emotional and sexual conflict. When those feelings are confusing, shame-filled, or overwhelming, especially in a child who lacks healthy boundaries, they cannot be acted on directly. Instead, the aggression gets buried, reshaped, and carried forward, waiting for a safer substitute.[4]

In the teenager's case, repeated childhood bedwetting led to intimate physical care from his mother that crossed emotional boundaries and triggered sexual arousal he did not understand. That combination of desire, shame, and anger had nowhere to go. Over time, the urge to punish and destroy the source of those feelings did not disappear, it simply shifted. The violence that followed was not really about the women he killed. It was about reenacting the same emotional conflict over and over, attempting to master it by controlling, degrading, and ultimately destroying stand-ins for the original figure. While this does not excuse his actions, it helps explain how an early, unresolved dynamic could become one of the central engines driving his later crimes.[4]

The older the teenager grew, the more sex occupied his thoughts… specifically the way his body felt when he touched himself. Unfortunately for him, his mother made it clear that masturbation was a worse sin even than rape.[2] There were a couple of neighbor girls that caught his attention and he did everything he could to see through their blinds and catch them undressing, but had no luck with that. He began "accidentally" brushing up against girls as he passed them but he made sure not to touch the same girl too often so they wouldn't be suspicious. One time, he took a younger cousin into the woods, put his hand up her skirt, and touched her between her legs,[2] No matter where he went or what he did, he couldn't escape his obsession with sex. It was an all-encompassing need, a flame that never seemed to extinguish.

In addition to his obsession with sex, the teenager had a fascination with hurting things. He and his brothers shot BB guns at birds behind their house but that only staved off the desire for so long. One day, while feeling sorry for himself and angry at the world, his family's cat wandered up to him. Instead of petting the cat like he normally did, the 13-year-old forced it into a nearby cooler, shut the lid, and walked away. The next day he came back to see what had happened with his experiment, finding the cat still in the cooler, dead, after having obviously attempted to claw his way out of the cooler.[2]

The teenager had been carrying a knife around in his pocket since he was about 11-years-old,[2] but didn't use it to harm anyone until he was 15 or 16. He was walking to an event at the school when he saw a young boy, about 6-years-old, standing near some bushes. He took his knife, stabbed the kid in the side, and ran away.

> *"Ah, he was playin' with a stick like, cowboys and Indians or somethin' like that. And, ah, he, ah, bent... bent down to pick up somethin' or somethin' and I just took the knife outta my pocket and stabbed him in the ah, side. He grabbed his side and ran away, and I ran up the hill..."*[3]

Later, he said he just wanted to see how stabbing worked and that the 6-year-old "was in the wrong place at the wrong time and I was at the right place at the right time I guess what you'd call it."[3]

The young man graduated high school at age 20 and then began a short career in the army. Before leaving, he married his high school sweetheart, Claudia. Theirs was a short-lived marriage that started unraveling almost before it even began. Within six months of the young man's overseas deployment, his wife met someone else and was living with him by the time the young man returned. Upon his return, the two attempted to reconcile and they moved in together again, which was not successful. Their divorce was finalized in January of 1972 and Claudia moved back in with her boyfriend, whom she eventually married. When interviewed later about their relationship, Claudia had nothing but positive things to report about the young man, saying he was a very social person and had a normal sex drive, things just didn't work out. The young man, however, was less positive, saying that upon his return from deployment Claudia was "living with several black men" and had become a "whore" who had given him genital warts.[5]

Overall, the young man's teenage years and early twenties were marked with a lot of sexual confusion, frustration, and overwhelming desires that filled him with guilt and anger. While it's not likely that any one of these experiences caused him to turn into the man he eventually became, they certainly played a significant role in his growth and development. Taken together, the 1960s and 70s were filled with frustration, confusion, and heartbreak, while we'll soon see that the 1980s were marked by more certainty and determination than ever.

CHAPTER 22

Less than a year after his divorce from Claudia, the young man married wife number two: Marcia. The start of their relationship was atypical, beginning when the boy pulled her over, impersonating a police officer. Marcia said he looked like a police officer so she pulled over, somehow managing not to be his first victim and ending up as his next wife instead.[1]

The two lived together for one year before getting married. From the start, the young man presented himself as damaged and misunderstood, telling Marcia he might not be able to have children due to venereal disease and speaking bitterly about his first wife, Claudia. That past relationship never really left the marriage. Even during intimacy, he sometimes used Claudia's name, a detail that left Marcia feeling unsettled and interchangeable rather than chosen.[1]

Their life together appeared ordinary on the surface. They rode bikes, attended both a Baptist and a Pentecostal church, fished, camped, and eventually had a son, Matthew, in 1975. Not long after Matthew was born, the young man became fanatical about religion. While they attended their Pentecostal church, he eagerly went door-to-door witnessing to people but would become irrationally angry when they shut their doors on him. At home, Marcia would frequently come home to the young man sitting on the couch with a

Bible on his lap, studying scripture and trying to learn more about his newfound religion.

The young man spent many weekends with his parents and kept much of his inner life closed off. He had no close friends, guarded his garage as a private space, and was frequently gone for long stretches of time, often returning dirty or wet with illogical or no explanations. Over time, Marcia began to feel less like a partner and more a roommate. In a later interview, she described feeling reduced to a housekeeper and sex object rather than a wife, and she noticed his preference for secrecy, isolation, and control.[1]

As time went on, troubling behavior became harder to explain away. The young man liked to sneak up on Marcia, frighten her, and place her in choke holds, framing it as play even when it crossed into fear. One night, after attending a party together where there was alcohol, he attacked her outside their home, wrapping his arms around her neck in what she later described as a police-style hold. When she fought back and demanded he call the police, he refused and tried to convince her someone else had done it. That moment marked a change in their relationship and Marcia was no longer able to convince herself that things were okay. By the end of the marriage, the young man's absences, secrecy, and need for dominance had turned their relationship into something tense and frightening, leaving Marcia with the growing realization that the man she married was far more dangerous than he appeared.[1]

Later on, after the man was caught and the police were tracking down victims and families, Marcia was asked if she could provide any assistance to their team. Not knowing what she could offer, she offered up what she could– several years' worth of destinations she and her ex-husband would frequent during intimate moments of their marriage. It turned out that she was able to pinpoint four locations where several clusters of the remains of the man's victims were found buried. While Marcia thought she had been there to experience a special moment of love with her husband, the man was getting off on knowing his victims lay just a few feet under where they were having sex.[1]

Between 1981 and 1984 when the man's marriage with Marcia had been over for mere months, he engaged in three separate relationships, sometimes at the same time. His relationship with his first girlfriend started innocently enough, but quickly accelerated and morphed into something new entirely. Throughout the entire relationship, the two engaged in frequent sexual acts– sometimes as many as three times per day– and it seemed as though the man's sexual appetite was impossible to sate. As time went on, the man started engaging in more violent sexual behavior, going beyond "typical" BDSM acts. He would bring wooden stakes on dates, drive them into the ground outside, and tie his girlfriend to them before having sex with her. Both times, while surely more aggressive than she had been expecting, the girl allowed it to happen and was untied as soon as she asked.[1]

The man's girlfriend described him as emotionally withdrawn and intensely private, with almost no friends outside of his family. He deferred nearly all decisions to her and seemed passive in daily life, but was overly dependent on the relationship itself. Over time, his constant need for closeness became overwhelming, and she eventually asked him to leave, which he did shortly before Christmas of 1981[1].

He started dating his second girlfriend right after breaking up with the first, although girlfriend number two was pretty sure he was dating multiple women during this time. Unlike the first, the man never asked his second girlfriend to engage in any untowardly sexual acts. He was mild-mannered and usually in control of his emotions, but he demonstrated a lack of self-esteem. His girlfriend felt that it was his mother's fault that he felt he was never able to satisfy or please anyone.[1]

On Christmas Eve 1981, the man approached girlfriend number two at a bar and visibly shaken, told her he had picked up a prostitute and had almost killed her. Before he could elaborate, others sat down at the table and the subject changed. Neither of them ever brought it up again. A few months later, the girl was approached by another woman who said she thought the man had been dating both of them at the same time and that she had contracted a sexually transmitted disease due to the prostitutes he was also sleeping with[1].

The man started dating girlfriend number three in January 1982, while he was still dating his second girlfriend. Their relationship moved quickly, but it was soon complicated by an STD diagnosis, which he refused to take responsibility for and instead blamed on her. Over the next year and a half, they continued seeing each other regularly, mostly at her home since she had children, and their social world remained small. He had very few friends outside of work, occasionally stopping for a beer with coworkers, and she came to realize he was not faithful after seeing other women at his house[1].

During their time together, the man spoke often and bitterly about his former wives, particularly his first. He appeared deeply wounded by those relationships and carried a simmering resentment, especially toward women he believed had betrayed him. Despite this, he usually presented as calm and even-tempered, rarely showing outward anger. Still, there were moments that unsettled her, including overhearing him say he could kill his ex-wife if he wanted to. Though he was attentive and gentle in the relationship and largely predictable in his routines, he showed a clear pattern of compartmentalizing women, expressing contempt for some while idealizing others. When she eventually called off their planned wedding in 1984, he showed little reaction and quickly replaced her, making her feel as though the relationship had been interchangeable rather than personal.

What none of these women knew was that while he was dating them, he was also engaging in far more nefarious acts. Between 1982 and 1984, the man murdered at least 42 women.[2] crossing a line he could never uncross.

CHAPTER 23

Gary Ridgeway, known nationwide as the "Green River Killer" claimed responsibility for 42 victims, with at least 12 more unaccounted for. He killed– mostly women and prostitutes– for 20 years before getting caught, the vast majority of those murders happening in the early 1980s.[1]

While he claimed not to remember his first murder,[2] the first victim Ridgeway was prosecuted for was named Wendy Lee Coffield, a 16-year-old who was last seen July 7, 1982.[1] Wendy had a difficult childhood and started sleeping with men around the age of 13, when she met an older teenager who she began a relationship with. The older boy moved in with Wendy and her mom, who at that point had also started sleeping with him. He became abusive to both mother and daughter, though, and Wendy ran away frequently to escape the chaos that the household had become. Around this time, she began sleeping with men for money as well as stealing from them so she could afford drugs and some semblance of the lifestyle she wanted. In early 1982, Wendy's mother moved to Washington and left Wendy to fend for herself. In July, Wendy visited her mother for the first and last time. She was found on July 15th strangled and dumped in the Green River.[3] And thus began the Green River Killer's stranglehold over the nation.

Early on, Ridgway insisted that his murders were never planned. He framed them as impulsive acts, claiming he only killed when he became overwhelmed with anger. He shifted blame onto the victims, saying their reactions during sex provoked him, whether they seemed uninterested or pressured him to finish quickly. According to Ridgway, these moments sent him into a physical rage where his body shook, his breathing faltered, and his thinking narrowed until everything felt blurred and out of control.[4] He even said there were a few times he had the opportunity to kill but didn't have the urge. "It could have been where I had a real good day at work. Somebody patted me on the back, 'you did a good job today,' which was a rarity. It could have been on my birthday.. Or maybe I just didn't have time to kill them and take them someplace."[4]

After Wendy Lee Coffield, the deaths accelerated. Over the next several years, women began disappearing along Pacific Highway South, many of them teenagers, many of them struggling with addiction, homelessness, or survival sex. Their bodies were later found dumped in clusters near rivers, wooded areas, and back roads Ridgeway knew intimately. Once police started connecting his victims, he began going out of his way to evade them by doing things like leaving cigarette butts and gum wrappers that didn't belong to him, changing his tires more frequently than needed, and cutting the victim's fingernails if they scratched him.[1] He also always wore gloves and didn't pick up prostitutes unless they were alone. One time he pulled a muscle dragging a body into the woods, and he claimed it was a work-related injury and collected workers compensation on it.[1]

Ridgeway's second victim was Deborah "Dub" Lynn Bonner, a 23-year-old prostitute. She had been dating her boyfriend Carl for several years and he also acted as her pimp, although she didn't think of him that way. She loved her "job" and doing what she did so she could support her boyfriend's lifestyle. Dub was attractive and known to others as a fun-loving and kindhearted person with a lot of friends. Sadly, July 25th was the last time she was seen alive and her body was found on August 12, 1982, soon to be known as the Green River Killer's second victim.[3]

As Ridgeway got going with his crimes in 1982, he mostly killed young girls and prostitutes after having sex with them. They were easy to pick up, their disappearances were slow to be reported due to their transient nature, and he often stole any money they had on them, too.[1] Between 1983 and 1984, the killings escalated dramatically and Ridgeway seemed to find his groove, so to speak. He murdered 40-42 women during this time frame, often killing several women per month. Most of Gary Ridgeway's victims were strangled, typically using their own clothing as a ligature. Many of the bodies were posed or revisited, with some buried and others left exposed, reflecting a disturbing pattern in how he treated the remains. Several of the victims were minors, though Ridgeway often minimized or outright denied their ages. Exact dates of death are frequently uncertain, particularly for victims whose remains were found skeletonized, making the timeline of his crimes difficult to reconstruct with precision.

Ridgeway was so difficult to track down because of the way he seemed to play with the people who were after him. Take Carol Ann Christenson, for example. Carol was 21 years old when she disappeared after leaving work on May 3, 1983; her body recovered five days later on May 8, 1983. She had been strangled to death, consistent with Ridgway's method, but what set her case apart was the way her body was arranged. The 21-year-old was found fully clothed with a paper bag over her head, two fish laid across her chest, a bottle of wine on her stomach, and sausages placed near her hands. Investigators initially questioned whether a different killer was responsible because of the bizarre arrangement, but later DNA evidence tied Ridgway to her murder, and he admitted killing her, claiming he posed the body to mislead detectives.[5]

All told, Ridgeway had at least 48 victims including Wendy Lee Coffield, Gisele Lovvorn, Debra Lynn Bonner, Marcia Fay Chapman, Cynthia Jean Hinds, Opal Charmaine Mills, Denise Bush, Terry R. Milligan, Mary Meehan, Debra Lorraine Estes, Shawnda Lee Summers, Shirley Sherrill, Colleen Brockman, Alma Ann Smith, Delores Laverne Williams, Gail Lynn Mathews, Marie Malvar, Andrea Childers, Sandra Kay Gabbert, Kimi-Kai Pitsor, Cheryl Lee Wims, Carol Ann Christensen, Martina Authorlee, Yvonne "Shelly" Antosh, Carrie Ann Rois, Constance Naon, Kelly Marie Ware, Tina Marie Thompson, April Buttram, Debbie May Abernathy, Tracy Winston, Maureen Feeney, Mary Sue Bello, Kim Lee Nelson, Pammy Annette Avent, Delise Plager, Cindy A. Smith, Lisa Yates, Mary West, Roberta J. Hayes, Patricia Yellowrobe, Linda Rule, and Marta Reeves, along with several unidentified victims known as Jane Doe B10, Jane Doe B16, Jane Doe B17, and Jane Doe B20.[7]

While the vast majority of Gary Ridgeway's victims were murdered in the mid-1980s, Ridgeway wasn't arrested until 2001– nearly 20 years later.[6] At the time, police had biological evidence from several victims, but DNA testing at the time was too limited to identify a suspect. Ridgway was interviewed multiple times during the original investigation and even took a polygraph, which he passed. He stayed on law enforcement's radar, but there was not enough evidence to charge him. In the late 1990s as new DNA testing techniques came on the scene, samples were able to be re-tested and Ridgeway was finally arrested, pleading guilty on November 5, 2003[6].

The Green River Killer's eventual arrest did not bring closure so much as it brought confirmation of what many families had feared for decades. The sheer length of time he was able to offend, often in plain sight, exposed deep limitations in investigative tools, social attitudes toward marginalized victims, and the assumptions law enforcement made about who looked like a killer. What followed his arrest was not relief, but reckoning. And with that reckoning came a fuller understanding of just how much damage had been done long before anyone was ready to name him for what he was.

CHAPTER 24

When you look at the way Gary Ridgeway grew up and some of the inclinations and leanings he had from the time he was young, nobody would have been surprised if he had grown up somewhat troubled. But what was it inside that caused him to become the monster he became, murdering at least 48 women? According to the prosecutors during his trial and presumably the psychologists who evaluated him, there was no mental illness he did or could have suffered from that would have provided an answer to the "why." Nothing that could have exonerated him from the blame for his offenses. During the interviews prior to and during his trial, Ridgeway showed no empathy, remorse, or care for what he had done. He couldn't even reliably recall the faces of his victims. He murdered because he chose to, because no one stopped him, and because it gratified him. Stripped of excuses and explanations, the motive is as simple and as disturbing as that.[1]

Despite this, there is an interesting correlation between Ridgeway's childhood and the Macdonald Triad, a theoretical framework that highlights recurring patterns seen in some violent offenders but is not a predictive or definitive model of future criminal behavior. First developed by Psychiatrist J. M. Macdonald in 1963, the Macdonald Triad is a theory that suggests fire-setting without clear motives, enuresis (bedwetting after age five), and animal cruelty create the perfect recipe for a future in serial murder. The connection between animal cruelty and violent crimes later in life is somewhat obvious, and studies have shown that while not all serial killers have a past in animal cruelty, most do. Fire-setting and animal cruelty also have an interesting correlation, as individuals who engaged in animal cruelty as kids were more likely to engage in fire-setting. Enuresis is an involuntary and non-violent act that doesn't seem to quite fit in this triad. However, some research has found that enuresis is present in individuals who have had traumatic experiences as children and engaged in behaviors such as sexual deviance, stealing, exposure to porn before age 12, fire-setting, etc. So while correlation doesn't equal causation, the presence of enuresis can be an indication of a troubled childhood and a predictor of violence in the future.[2]

Of the three components in the Macdonald Triad, Ridgeway had enuresis and engaged in fire-setting all throughout his youth. While enuresis seems to be the weakest link in the Triad, it likely plays the largest role in the trajectory of Ridgeway's life, as that is what led to the sexual abuse from his mother and feelings of shame and self-loathing that trickled in in the immediate aftermath. Well into Ridgeway's teenage years, when he was fully capable of cleaning himself after wetting the bed, his mother was still scrubbing his genitals on an almost daily basis.[3] Naturally, this made him feel turned on, ashamed, and angry. Research has shown lethal outcomes due to this kind of abuse, with 70% of serial killers having a past of some kind of parental abuse.[2] Children who grow up in abusive environments may later seek to replicate those same dysfunctional attachment patterns, attempting to regain control by inflicting the fear and pain they once endured onto others.[2] This may help to give a small glimpse into the mind of Gary Ridgeway, a man who was sexually abused by his domineering mother and who then went on to sexually abuse, dominate, and murder prostitutes.

Another hurdle Ridgeway struggled to move past was his IQ and dyslexia. Low intelligence alone doesn't cause violence, nor does it predict a future in violent criminal behavior with any certainty. However, research shows that lower childhood IQ is associated with a significantly higher risk of a wide range of mental health disorders across an individual's life, which includes antisocial behavior, substance use disorders, depression, and personality pathology. One explanation is that cognitive limitations reduce a person's ability to regulate emotions, problem-solve under stress, and foresee consequences, skills that are critical buffers against maladaptive behavior.[4]

When low IQ intersects with chronic stressors like parental rejection, abuse, or persistent humiliation, the risk escalates. Research suggests that children with lower cognitive ability are more likely to experience repeated failure and social marginalization, which in turn increases anger, resentment, and emotional numbing over time… all of which are clearly present in Ridgeway. Children who experience this often internalize the belief that they are defective or inferior, a belief that can later manifest as hostility toward others or a need to regain control through domination. In this context, intelligence is not the cause, but it is a vulnerability factor, one that shapes how a child absorbs and responds to the world around them.[4]

What's important to make clear here is that many individuals with low IQs grow into nonviolent, law-abiding adults.[4] What differentiates outcomes is not intelligence itself, but environment, attachment, and opportunity. In Ridgeway's case, his low IQ was met not with protection or accommodation, but with criticism and neglect. Over time, those repeated experiences taught him a dangerous lesson:

that he was powerless, unseen, and fundamentally different. Psychology tells us that when those beliefs harden early, they rarely disappear on their own.

At the end of the day, while there are hints of potential mental disorders that can be pinned on Ridgeway, according to him, his biggest problem was he simply didn't care. When asked to rate his level of evil on a scale of one to ten, he gave himself a three because he killed the women quickly instead of torturing them first.[1] In interviews during his trial, he told the forensic psychologist that he had never fantasized about killing anyone except "maybe" his mom before the first time he killed. Later, he added that he also wanted to kill his second wife, whom he consistently blamed for problems in his life: "…If I would have killed her then it's possible that it might have changed my life. I'd only have one instead of 50 plus."[5] He always dreamt of sexual dominance of women but murder was never a part of the plan. The first time he killed a woman he had just slept with, his main thoughts were of not knowing what to do with the body and relief that he didn't have to drive her home anymore. Despite the lack of foresight into what he called his "career," he beamed with pride when talking about everything he had "accomplished" afterward, hoping that one day a Seattle-based true crime writer would write about his story (apologies from this Midwest-based true crime writer).[5]

On November 5, 2003, Gary Ridgeway pleaded guilty to 48 counts of aggravated first-degree murder. He was sentenced to 48 life terms and was fined $10,000 for each of the 48 lives he took.[6] Nevertheless, no sentence, no fine, and no number of years spent behind bars can ever account for the lives Gary Ridgway took or the devastation left in their absence.

PART 6

POWER OVER LIFE AND DEATH

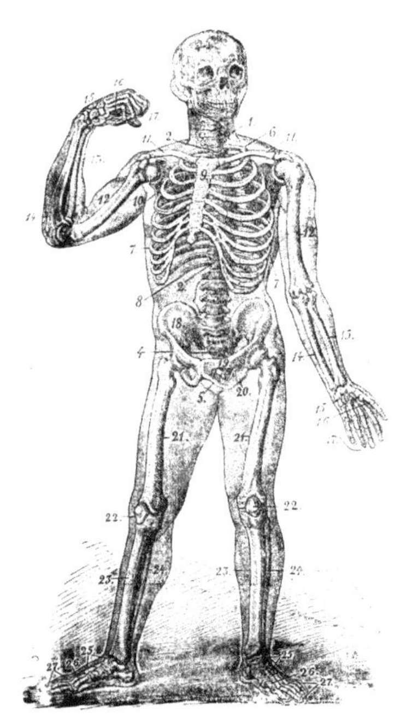

CHAPTER 25

It's a sunny afternoon in 1950s Kansas. A young boy kneels on the floor of his grandparents' kitchen, carefully rolling strands of twine into a growing ball, the threads tangling around his fingers. Outside, the wind rattles the windows, but he barely notices. His brothers chase each other through the yard, laughing and shouting, while his mother lounges nearby, absorbed in a magazine. He feels a thrill at the control he holds in his hands, the ability to bind and shape the twine exactly as he wants. Even at this young age, he senses a fascination with power and order that he cannot yet explain.

Born on March 9, 1945 in Columbus, Kansas, the boy was the oldest of four with an unremarkable childhood, despite his mom having fallen off a horse while pregnant with him and then dropping him on his head when he was 6-8 months old. His parents were young– just 20 and 23– and he spent much of his childhood at his grandparents' house around the corner. His grandparents were supportive, loving, and provided a stable upbringing for the boy. When he would cower during thunderstorms, his grandma made up a story about the loud noise simply being a potato wagon crossing a bridge and all the potatoes falling out.[1]

The boy's grandma was not overly friendly and her head always seemed to be in the clouds, but she was a constant presence who was very helpful and the boy particularly loved her long hair that she would tie up with ribbons. His grandpa was a barber who loved playing pool, drinking beer, and playing dominoes. While staying with his grandparents, his mother's personality and habits seemed to change in a way that was interesting but not overly concerning to the boy. She smoked, drank, and watched TV rather than helping with the kids, almost reverting to her younger self due to being in her parents' home. She always seemed to prefer having someone other than herself take care of her own kids, so the boy never felt very close to her.[1]

Life was pretty normal for the boy. His parents slowly climbed up the ladder in their careers of choice, moving the family from poor and in the lower class to solidly in the middle class. They moved around Kansas a couple different times when he was young, but when they finally stuck in Seneca, he was able to make some good friends such as John, Allen, and Bobby. His dad was a hard worker and built them a large garden and a chicken house; eventually part of the boy's chores was to water and feed the chickens and clean up after them.[1]

In elementary school he struggled with academics and had trouble reading and writing, but enjoyed the extra-curriculars. The boy joined Boy Scouts and learned survival skills such as how to tie knots and start fires. One day while with a friend, he touched a used but still-smoldering cigar butt to a cardboard box and the box lit on fire, starting to spread toward the dead grass nearby. It was an accident but it also excited him to see how quickly the fire started and spread. He was able to stop it and was ashamed, partly at the fact that he had started it and partly at the fact that he had been so excited by the thrill of it.[1]

Outside of academics, the boy's interactions with his younger brothers became another important arena for learning about leadership, control, and play. The boy and his younger brothers got along well, playing typical boyhood games like Cowboys and Indians where they took turns playing different characters. When it was the boy's turn to be the prisoner and he was captured and tied up, he found he enjoyed the feeling of being tied up. They fought occasionally as all siblings do, but never picked on each other for the heck of it. It was important to the boy that he be a good role model for his brothers. He loved being the leader and felt a semblance of pride at being the "superior one."[1] One summer, the brothers became obsessed with breaking the world record for the world's largest ball of twine, which had been started in 1953 by Frank Stoeber.[3] They made a bet to see who could create the biggest ball and all began seeking out any type of string or twine they could find. The boy continued collecting string and growing his ball for years, sharing later that the "feeling of tying up loose ends with the string" felt good to him.[1]

There are a couple of memories that stayed with the boy his entire life. One of which was a story his grandma told him about his older cousin, Larry, the favorite grandchild and therefore the one with the most toys. One day, Larry was playing with a friend near the creek. When he got back home and was asked where his friend was, he told them he didn't know. Shortly thereafter, Larry's friend was found dead in the creek.[1] Another event that stuck with the boy was finding a toy on a sidewalk and getting yelled at by his mother for stealing it, even though he insisted it wasn't on anyone's property. She made him feel like a thief, which in turn made him feel lonely and upset. Later, he says, he intentionally took things but he learned from his mistakes and kept them secret.[1]

While the boy's mother and her parents were not Christian, his dad was a strong Christian and so the whole family was active in the Lutheran church they attended. One day while at church, the boy felt a tug from the Holy Spirit and decided to become an altar boy or "acolyte." In his own words, he was "sharply focused on being good"[1] and made sure to be on his best behavior at all times. He would become extremely upset when he heard other kids take the Lord's name in vain, use swear words, and engage in risky sexual activities or drug use.[1]

Despite his outwardly pious behavior, a hidden side of the boy's mind was already harboring dark impulses he could never share. From the age of about three he started seeing a "monster" that would urge him to do things he knew he shouldn't; he claims it was because of his "little friend" that he always knew he would end up a murderer.

After he found his mother sobbing with her hand stuck in the couch after having caught her wedding band on a spring, for the first time ever he experienced a strange feeling in his stomach and groin. The memory replayed in his mind thousands of times, but he often replaced his mom with various women who were bound to the couch and in tremendous pain. As a pre-teen boy he started masturbating but when his mother found out she beat him, instilling in him that juvenile belief that "If you masturbate God will come and kill you."[1] She held the boy's hands behind his back and used a belt to whip him, which hurt but also turned him on. Throughout his childhood, his mother used a belt to whip the boys when they misbehaved, and though it was painful, it became a game to them as they raced through the house to avoid the whip.[1]

Some of the boy's favorite clothing items from his childhood were his mother's satin slips and his grandmother's hair ribbons. He frequently masturbated while thinking of other women in those items, bound up with the twine from his ball. The women in his family were never victims of his fantasy crimes, but they were the source of his sexual fantasies. By the time he was in 6th grade he was fantasizing about bondage, and just two years later he was drawing detailed pictures depicting bondage situations and "doing self-bondage."[1] His difficulty in school made him feel shy around girls, which made him feel angry and want to both possess them and punish them. He frequently fantasized about tying them up and then either killing them or rescuing them, not really caring about the ending and leaving him with the sense that he was in control either way.

The boy's self-bondage increased exponentially as he continued fantasizing about his female neighbors and classmates. Every chance he got he would find himself in his barn, basement, or bathroom and either asphyxiate himself by tying himself at his midsection or tie a noose around his neck for a sexual release. Around this time, age 10 or 11, he also began spying on girls through their windows, dreaming about what he would do to them if he got the courage to break into their homes. In 4th grade he lost recess privileges almost daily because he refused to drink the required white milk, so he stayed inside alone and began drawing increasingly violent and sexual images of girls. During this time he would also fantasize about his "DTPG room" (Death to Pretty Girls), a barn that had wooden beams and chains, and that he could fully terrorize and dominate females.

The boy's first experience with death was at a young age, as is typical of young children born on a farm. The chickens were raised to be slaughtered and eaten, so standing around watching a chicken be tied up and then having his head cut off was a common and alluring occurrence for the boy. Even when he wasn't the one doing the binding and killing, the boy got a thrill out of that control, feeling as though "the one who holds the power over life and death is in charge."[1] Around this time he also started killing cats and dogs around the farm by hanging or strangling them.[2] He later came back and said he never killed dogs, but he admitted multiple times to killing cats, saying he felt like cats had supernatural powers and he had a strong desire to control them.[1]

Even with these early exposures to life and death, his upbringing was otherwise stable and free of the abuse often seen in serial killers. This underscores an important truth: experiencing abuse does not predetermine a person to become a killer, and conversely, an absence of abuse does not guarantee they won't. Whether shaped more by nature or nurture, the boy's early life contained all the elements that, in time, would encourage him to develop into the violent criminal he ultimately became.

CHAPTER 26

On November 15, 1959, the Clutter family of Holcomb, Kansas, was brutally murdered in their home. Herb and Bonnie Clutter, along with their teenage children Nancy and Kenyon, were bound, shot, and left for dead in a crime that shocked the small farming community.[1] That same day, the 14-year-old was riding in the car with a girl he had a massive crush on. When the story of the murder came on the radio, he was enthralled. He instantly pictured himself binding up the girl sitting next him and killing her in exactly the same manner as Herb, Bonnie, Nancy, and Kenyon.[2]

That same year, the teenager did his first breaking and entering at his high school, where he didn't steal or deface anything but he rifled through a girl's desk and drew a line on the blackboard, simply enjoying the power he felt. He got bolder and began breaking and entering local homes that he knew would be empty, going through girls' intimates, stealing them, and later using them to masturbate. The teenager's favorite fantasy these days featured an actress who had been on *The Mickey Mouse Club* when he was younger but who had somehow grown into a beautiful young woman. He imagined all sorts of violent sexual fantasies involving imprisonment, torture, and acts of self-gratification. His resentment toward women, particularly those he perceived as having power over him, fused into an experience where dominance and vulnerability existed at the same time.[2]

Between high school graduation and his early-mid 20s, the teenager's "Dark Side," as he called it, wasn't active. He was so focused on school, dating, and getting his career started, that he didn't have time for hobbies. In 1963 the 18-year-old bought his first car and dated his first girl; he went to movies, listened to the radio, and lived his best teenage-boy life. He experienced his first heartbreak when he was turned down by a girl he had been trying to impress, and debated killing himself in a crash later that evening as he was driving between 80 and 100mph. He bounced back pretty quickly, though, and dated girls regularly to get past the heartbreak. The one time he got close to letting his "Dark Side" out was when he was working one night and some people tried to break in. He called the cops and then after work he drove around town until he found their cars and slashed their tires.[2]

In his free time, the boy enjoyed looking through "detective magazines," mid-20th-century pulp crime publications that blended sensationalized crime stories with provocative imagery. Though framed as journalism or cautionary tales, these magazines often featured bound or distressed women, providing socially acceptable access to bondage and domination imagery that reinforced his emerging fantasies of power and control.[3] The teenager later admitted that he was addicted to these magazines and they fueled his desire to use bondage to control beautiful women in distress. They also inspired him to create his own "hit-kit," a collection of tools supposedly used by criminals to carry out assaults, kidnappings, or murders. He had no one in mind when he created it, but "had a feeling" he needed to have one.[2]

After initially dropping out of college, the young man returned to school largely due to pressure from friends around the time he turned 21. On the surface, he appeared to be doing what many college-aged men did at the time. He dated frequently, attended parties, and drank heavily, blending in easily with his peers. Beneath that normalcy, however, his compulsions intensified. He began breaking into dorm rooms and apartments, stealing small items he believed were insignificant, not for need but for the thrill. He convinced himself he was still in control, believing he would never cross "the line" because his conscience would intervene. In reality, each theft quietly reinforced the excitement of intrusion, secrecy, and getting away with it.[2]

Another hobby quietly taking shape during this period was the young man's fixation on contemporary serial killers. He read books and magazine articles obsessively, returning to the same stories over and over. His favorite was Albert DeSalvo, the Boston Strangler, whose murders occurred between 1962 and 1964 and involved the sexual strangulation of women in their homes. He also followed Richard Speck, who murdered eight student nurses in Chicago in 1966; Charles Whitman, who carried out the University of Texas tower shooting in 1966; Charles Manson and the Tate-LaBianca murders of 1969; and the Zodiac Killer, who terrorized Northern California between 1968 and 1974 with taunting letters and coded messages. These cases fascinated him not just for the violence, but for the notoriety each killer achieved.[2]

DeSalvo, in particular, became a model rather than just a subject of interest. The young man read *The Boston Strangler* repeatedly, watched the film adaptation, and began to see himself reflected in DeSalvo's dual life. During his earliest murders, he even wore green pants and a green sweatshirt to mimic DeSalvo, a deliberate choice that blurred the line between fantasy and action. These stories were not cautionary tales to him. They functioned as scripts, rehearsed again and again, reinforcing the idea that violence could coexist with normalcy and that anonymity, planning, and ritual could sustain both.[2]

After college, the young man was recruited into the Air Force and trained as a communications specialist rather than a combat soldier. His job focused on maintaining military communication systems, which meant climbing telephone poles, installing antennas, and ensuring reliable transmission of signals between bases. This technical, physically demanding work required precision and strict adherence to procedure. He was eventually sent overseas, including an assignment in Okinawa, where he performed the same duties while adjusting to military life far from home, further reinforcing the structure, routine, and isolation that would become familiar to him.[2]

While in the service, the young man continued creating and collecting pictures of pretty girls in bondage, as well as practicing self-bondage when he was alone in his room, but his behavior remained private for the time being. He had sex for the first time when he was 22 with a prostitute and had a subpar experience. Later on, he paid more money to tie up the prostitutes so he could get off on seeing them struggle, and he had a much more enjoyable experience.[2]

The young man's teenage years and early twenties were fairly PG-rated, relative to where he'd go in the mid-1970s. He had his fantasies and acted on them in the privacy of any room he could find, but didn't branch out beyond paying extra for bondage and breaking into homes to steal forgettable items. At this stage, his deviance remained largely contained, rehearsed in secrecy and rationalized as harmless, giving him the false sense that he was still in control of where his impulses would ultimately lead.

CHAPTER 27

After being honorably discharged from the Air Force in August 1970, the man met a woman named Paula and fell head over heels in love with her. She was beautiful, steady, and well-liked by his parents, and for the first time he could clearly picture a conventional future for himself. He married her in May of 1971, convinced he had found the life he was supposed to live. During their courtship and early marriage, his attention shifted toward building a stable adulthood. He worked steadily, began taking college courses again at a local school, and focused on being a dependable husband. He took pride in supporting Paula and presenting himself as a responsible young man with plans and direction.[1]

Outwardly, he blended seamlessly into normal life. He was employed, married, and moving forward in ways that appeared healthy and grounded. In this season, he rarely dwelled on what he privately referred to as his "Dark Side," believing it to be dormant or manageable. Marriage, work, and routine gave him the illusion that those urges belonged to an earlier version of himself, one that had been outgrown. He still enjoyed the fantasy of restraining a girl and watching her struggle, but Paula said "no" when he asked if he could tie her up, and their sex life was good enough, so he never asked again. For a time, he truly believed love, structure, and responsibility had placed him firmly on the right side of the line.[1]

The cracks started to show in early 1971 when Paula got in a bad car accident while heading in for work. She lost control on a bridge and was rushed to the hospital with what ended up being a broken back. While the man was driving from school to the hospital, he stopped at a drugstore to get some gifts for Paula, and happened to notice a bookstore next door. On a whim, the man decided to quickly check out the bookstore before heading to see Paula and he came across more of the detective magazines he used to read obsessively in his teens. Over the course of the next several weeks that Paula was in the hospital, the man stopped at that bookstore every chance he got to browse through and buy more of the detective magazines, hiding them in secret places around his house. His focus at school and on the supposed love of his life started slipping as his attention turned to the magazines.[1]

Once Paula healed well enough to go home, the man found other places to hide his magazines, read them in private, and bind himself continuously for the high. He began seeking out increasingly isolated locations where he could carry out these behaviors, including abandoned bridges, barns, and empty houses. There, he rehearsed elaborate self-restraint rituals involving ropes, nooses, and props, often bringing weapons and a prepared "hit kit," later admitting that had the opportunity presented itself, his violent offenses could have begun years earlier.[1]

The cracks really started widening in 1974. In early 1973, he got a good enough job working on the production line at one of the local aircraft manufacturer's facilities. The couple was happy, spending time volunteering at church, building relationships in the community, and dreaming of buying a new home and starting a family. Nine months later, he was laid off and everything changed.[1]

With nothing but time on his hands his years of fantasizing and planning came to fruition. One day, the man noticed a woman leaving to take her children to school. For no obvious reason other than boredom, he began stalking the woman – Julia Otero – and her family. He learned where they lived, what time the boys and father were gone, and when the women of the house would be alone. He fantasized about them in private and made plans to carry out his fantasies for the first time ever.

The Otero family was a closeknit, loving family who were active in their community. 38-year-old Joseph Otero was described by those who knew him as outgoing and jovial, while his 34-year-old wife Julie was recalled as caring and devoted to her five children: Charlie (15), Danny (14), Carmen (13), Josephine (11), and Joey (9). Their home was one where their children played freely and were known to others in the neighborhood, and even decades after the murders, neighbors still remembered the family fondly.[3]

On January 15, 1974 between about 7 and 7:30am, the man cut the phone lines to the house and waited by the back door for someone in the Otero family to inevitably "let" him in. Once the youngest Otero, Joey, opened the door, the man held him up at gunpoint and entered the home. Joseph and Julie were home with their two youngest kids, Joey and Josephine, while their oldest three were at school. The man confronted the family and tried to control them, at one point telling them to lie down and even moving the family into a bedroom. Once inside and after making one of the kids put the dog outside, he bound all four family members with rope while still holding them at gunpoint.[4]

The man knew Joseph had been in a car accident recently and had cracked a rib, so he made sure to lay a pillow down for his head to make him as comfortable as possible. He was already planning on killing the family because they had seen his face and could ID him, but he didn't want to extend the pain any more than he had to. He started on Joseph by putting a bag over his head and a cord around his neck, but, having never strangled anyone before, he didn't know how much pressure to use or how long it would take. Joseph was able to tear a hole in the plastic bag that had been placed over his head, so the man added another bag and clothing to ensure asphyxiation.[4]

He then strangled Julie until he thought she was dead, and put a plastic bag over Joey's head, leading to a death similar to that of his dad's. At some point Julie briefly regained consciousness, and the man strangled her again with a cord. After killing the parents and Joey, he took Josephine to the basement and hung her from a pipe. While he didn't engage in any sexual assault of the family members, he later told the court that he had "sexual fantasies" after he had finished hanging Josephine. Afterward, he "cleaned up" the house, taking a few items like a radio and watch, then left in the family car, which he abandoned at a nearby store before walking back to his own vehicle.[4]

The feeling that came after that first killing was like nothing the man had ever experienced. It was exhilarating– a rush he wanted to feel over and over again.[1] His "Dark Side" had officially come out and it seemed that he would never be able to push it down again. And why should he want to?

CHAPTER 28

Dennis Rader, nicknamed the "BTK Killer," gained notoriety from 1974 to 2005 when he bound, tortured, and killed at least ten people in Wichita, Kansas. For decades, he lived an unassuming life as a husband, father, and community member, all while meticulously planning and executing his crimes. His ability to compartmentalize the ordinary aspects of his life from his violent urges made him nearly invisible to authorities and neighbors alike. It wasn't until 2005, when a calculated communication with the media and law enforcement finally led to his arrest, that the full scope of his crimes, and the decades of terror he inflicted, was revealed to the public.

The Oteros were Rader's first unfortunate victims and those murders gave him a rush he had never experienced. After escaping, he watched the news and stored newspaper clippings for months, getting high off of the chase, the notoriety, and the knowledge that law enforcement wasn't any closer to finding him than they were when they started. After a couple of months, though, it was no longer enough. He needed more.

On April 4th of that same year, after picking out and stalking his next victim- Kathryn Bright- Rader made his move again. Ensuring Kathryn was not home, he broke in and waited for her to arrive, surprised when she showed up with her brother, Kevin. Rader stabbed and strangled Kathryn to death, and attempted to do the same to her brother but failed. He noted later that he must have used ropes he found at the Oteros because "if I had brought my stuff Kevin would probably be dead."[1]

When Rader saw Kevin escaping out the side of Kathryn's house, he thought for sure he would be caught. Soon the police had a good enough description for a fairly accurate artist rendering of Rader, but no one came for him. There was a lot of discussion about whether the two home invasions were connected, but ultimately it was decided that they likely were not, because the MO was so different. Shortly after this, he chose a new victim and began stalking her, but once breaking into her house and realizing it was full of more men's items than women's, he lost interest and left.[2]

On October 22, 1974, Rader called a columnist at the local newspaper and told him to go to the public library and look inside a specific book where he would find details about the Otero murders. At the time, there were men being held who were suspected of committing the Otero murders. Rader, whether out of respect for the federal funding being wasted or, more likely, not wanting someone else to get the credit, told the police they had the wrong guys. In his letter, he wrote, "I did it all by myself and with no one's help…" He went on to say he couldn't help himself but he also couldn't turn himself in because the police would laugh at him. He also instructed them on his nickname: B.T.K.: Bind them, Torture them, Kill them.[2]

There was a lull from 1975 to 1977, during which time Rader's wife Paula gave birth to their child, Brian. While there is no documented information about Paula's recovery, it can be assumed that she healed enough to go back to her normal life. Rader continued going to church, attending community events, and spending time with his family, presenting the image of a devoted husband and father. He doted on Brian, thrilled by the milestones of fatherhood, yet behind closed doors he maintained his secret life—reading detective magazines filled with bondage and violence, and practicing self-bondage in private, keeping the darkness that had always driven him carefully hidden from the world.[2]

On March 17, 1977, Rader's terrorization of Wichita started again with 24-year-old Shirley Vian as victim number six. He tied Shirley and her kids up, locked the kids in another room, and proceeded to put a bag over Shirley's head and strangle her. On December 8th of the same year, he broke into the home of 25-year-old Nancy Fox and strangled her with a belt.[1]

Following the murders of Shirley and Nancy, Rader hit another lull, likely waiting excitedly to see if he would reach the same notoriety as previous serial killers such as the Boston Strangler or Zodiac. He soon sent his local newspaper a poem he had painstakingly written about Shirley, calling her "Shirleylocks" and talking about her death. When the newspaper failed to mention BTK, he grew frustrated that he wasn't getting the fame he deserved and wrote another poem–this time about Nancy– and a letter. In the letter, he expressed disdain for law enforcement for allegedly not letting the news talk about the killings. He said, "How many do I have to kill before I get a name in the paper or some national attention?" Then he went on to scoff at the police for believing "all those deaths are not related" and provided several more nicknames the news was welcome to call him in their coverage of his crimes.[2]

On June 13, 1978, Rader's daughter, Kerri, was born. In the months that followed, he appeared to withdraw from active killing while continuing to nurture his fantasies. By 1979, those fantasies had shifted toward stalking. Anna Williams, a 63yearold widow in Wichita, became a subject of Rader's stalking in April 1979. He waited inside her home for her return, intending to kill her, but left when she did not come back on her usual schedule. Two months later he sent her stolen personal items and a poem entitled "Oh Anna, Why Didn't You Appear?," showing how close she had come to becoming another BTK victim. The poem, a drawing of a woman being sexually violated and bound, and a few items taken from her home were also sent to the local news channel.[3]

Rader paused his murder spree until April 27, 1985, when he murdered his neighbor, 53-year-old Marine Hedge. The crimes continued with the September 16, 1986 killing of 28yearold Vicki Wegerle, whom Rader strangled inside her residence, and culminated with his last known victim, 62yearold Dolores Davis, whom he murdered on January 19, 1991, by strangulation using pantyhose, then relocated her body to a rural area.[1]

After the murder of Dolores Davis, Rader "retired" from killing, and the case ran cold. Then, on January 11, 2004, the local paper published an article about the Otero murders that had occurred nearly 30 years prior. This inspired Rader to start his cat-and-mouse games again by writing another letter to the police taunting them for not being able to catch him.[4] A few months later, he sent them a word puzzle featuring clues like "prowl" and "fantasies." While the note lacked his typical signature, careful observers later noticed that the letters R-A-D-E-R were arranged around the numbers 6220, revealing the killer's own street address. After a few more back-and-forth correspondences with law enforcement where Rader sent more pictures and items from his victims, he was finally caught by his own games. He sent a floppy disc to the cops with hidden information that also included metadata sharing exactly who and where he was. He was caught.[3]

On June 17, 2005, Dennis Rader pleaded guilty to ten counts of first-degree murder and provided explicit details about how he committed each one. Two months later he was sentenced to ten consecutive life terms in prison, for a minimum of 175 years without the possibility of parole.[3] BTK's reign was officially over.

CHAPTER 29

Dennis Rader was a serial killer who craved attention and notoriety and demonstrated this through his communications with the press and law enforcement, eventually getting him caught. After being interviewed extensively by psychologists as well as evaluated by millions of arm-chair detectives, doctors, and psychiatrists, Rader was diagnosed with Antisocial Personality Disorder (ASPD), Narcissistic Personal Disorder (NPD), and Obsessive-Compulsive Disorder (OCD).[1]

ASPD is characterized by a long-term pattern of disregard for the rights of others, impulsivity, deceitfulness, and lack of remorse for harmful actions. Individuals with ASPD often violate social norms and laws, act irresponsibly, and may engage in aggressive or criminal behavior.[1] OCD is marked by persistent, unwanted thoughts (obsessions) and repetitive behaviors or mental acts (compulsions) performed to reduce anxiety caused by these thoughts. Both disorders can interfere significantly with a person's daily life and relationships.[2]

Narcissistic Personality Disorder, meanwhile, involves a pervasive pattern of grandiosity, a need for excessive admiration, an inflated sense of self-importance, and a lack of empathy. Individuals with NPD may exploit others to achieve their goals, be preoccupied with fantasies of unlimited success or power, and have a strong sense of entitlement. The disorder can cause significant impairment in social, occupational, or other important areas of functioning.[3]

However, while the term "narcissist" is often used casually in everyday conversation, true NPD is a serious psychiatric condition diagnosed only when a consistent and pervasive pattern of these behaviors is present. Misusing the label can be harmful because it minimizes the experiences of people who genuinely struggle with the disorder and can lead to misunderstandings about mental health. It can also stigmatize normal self-interest or confidence, turning everyday disagreements or personality clashes into exaggerated judgments about someone's character. Using the term accurately is important both for respecting those with the disorder and for fostering a more nuanced understanding of human behavior.

Take Dennis Rader, for example. He was so profoundly self-centered that all he cared about was his own experience of the world. His daughter wrote a book in 2019 called *"A Serial Killer's Daughter: My Story of Faith, Love, and Overcoming"* all about how much pain and suffering she has been through due to her father's crimes, and the first thing Rader said in a letter correspondence was, "Did you see my name in the paper?" The only thing he has ever wanted was to leave a legacy. He wanted to be the best of the best in serial killing.[6]

Renowned Forensic Psychologist and author of the book *"Confession of a Serial Killer: The Untold Story of Dennis Rader, the BTK Killer,"* (the book much of this information was pulled from) Dr. Katherine Ramsland, sent Rader the book, *"The Anatomy of Violence"* by Adrian Raine so he could reflect on his own mental and behavioral traits. With a mix of curiosity and self-analysis, Rader attributed some of his tendencies to biological factors, such as a low heart rate, possible brain irregularities from a childhood injury, and a hyper-reactive dopamine reward system, which he believed made him prone to seeking intense gratification despite risks. He identified patterns in his own behavior consistent with psychopathy, antisocial tendencies, and obsessive reward-seeking, noting his compulsions for bondage, sexualized fantasies, and meticulous planning of his crimes.[5]

Rader also contrasted himself with the stereotypical serial killer, acknowledging he was not abused or neglected as a child and received love and support from his parents. He recognized the interplay of nature and nurture, suggesting that biological predispositions combined with social context, like exposure to media and early bondage interests, shaped his development into a killer. He compared himself to the psychological profiles in Raine's book, and even questioned how his childhood experiences and genetics contributed to his later violent behavior. Ultimately, he seemed to be fascinated by his own pathology, analyzing it almost as an experiment while acknowledging the compulsions and obsessions that drove his crimes.[5]

What's interesting about Dennis Rader is how well he was able to hide his true self. He had a wife, two kids, a work crew, a church, and an entire community fooled into believing he was the cream of the crop– a real stand-up guy who anyone would be lucky to have in their corner. At the time of his arrest he was the acting President of his Lutheran church's congregation. Shocked about his conviction, his pastor said, "He was a very pleasant man to be around. He was there every Sunday. I could depend on him to handle the sound system, to usher whenever we needed it. He engaged the members of the congregation in conversation, was willing to joke with people, but not an outgoing, boisterous kind of person."[7]

Dr. Ramsland called Rader's particular kind of narcissism "Narcissistic Immunity," which refers to a person's tendency to resist criticism or accountability because their inflated sense of self-worth and entitlement shields them from acknowledging mistakes or feeling genuine remorse. Ramsland noted that "while ordinary narcissists possess a smug sense of superiority that allows them to thoughtlessly exploit others for their own gain, some killers go so far as to believe that their victims were "privileged" to have been in their orbit."[5] Such was the case with Dennis Rader. He was driven by an intense need for total control and a belief that he was uniquely destined and intellectually superior, especially compared to those trying to catch him.

At the end of the day, Rader's need for complete control and notoriety and his belief in his infallibility was so overwhelming that he assumed he was eventually discovered by the very cops he thought were too dumb to ever figure him out.

PART 7

THE SPECIAL OLYMPICS OF CHURCHES

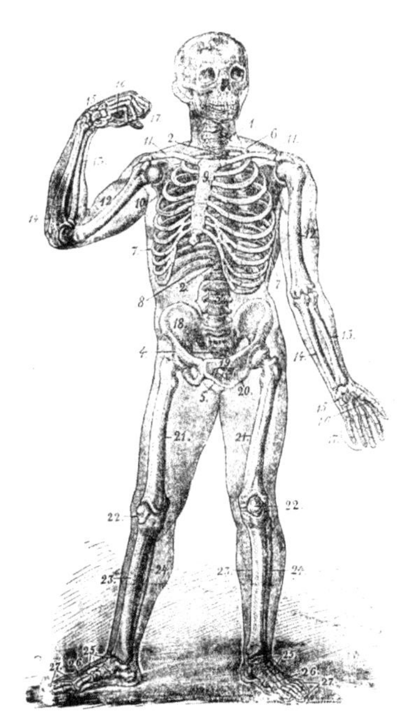

CHAPTER 30

It's a cloudy day in the Midwest and a young girl is walking her dog through her wealthy, gated community, knowing she is in a safe neighborhood and doesn't have anything to worry about except getting her dog some exercise. Out of the corner of her eye, she notices a sudden movement that makes her pause. When she looks up, she sees a boy hanging upside down from the second-story window of one of the nicer houses in the neighborhood, a hand clasping his ankle. She gasps, picks up her pace, and hurries home, telling no one what she saw.

November 22, 1943 was a chilly, 38 degree day in Ohio when the boy decided to make his debut appearance in the world to two parents who weren't that excited about him or each other. His father was a skilled craftsman working as a tool-and-die maker and his mother, a beautiful woman of creole descent, was a beautician. They were wealthy, but money was about the only problem they didn't have.[1]

The boy's mother was reportedly an alcoholic and his father was a "ferocious disciplinarian"[1] who his mother later accused of "gross neglect of duty."[1] In 1945, the couple gave birth to their second child, a son named Terry. As young boys, the brothers appeared to have a relatively typical sibling relationship, alternating between play and physical conflict. They fought as often as they played, which in itself was not unusual. However, as they grew older, the balance shifted and the conflict escalated, becoming more frequent and more intense. Notably, much of their aggression was directed not toward each other but toward their father.[1] This shared adversary appeared to create a form of bonding rooted in mutual resentment, where hostility toward the same individual temporarily aligned them, even as their relationship continued to deteriorate over time.

In 1946, the boys' parents went through a contentious divorce and they ended up in their mother's custody. Their mother remarried almost instantly, and would remarry another two times after that over the next 26 years before she killed herself in 1970. During the time the boys lived with their mother, life was unpredictable. They never knew how she was going to react or what version of their mother they would see at any given day or time. They had to walk on eggshells, lest they unknowingly provoke a reaction and awaken the beast within. Because of her emotional volatility and lack of functional regulation skills, the boys were never able to learn what true love and intimacy from a parent looks like, or how to read typical social cues.[2]

By the time the boy started school at around age six, their mother decided she didn't want the kids anymore and sent them back to live with their father.[3] There, their new stepmother took over child-rearing responsibilities[2] and while they didn't get along with her, their relationship with their father was even worse. The boy had been wetting his bed at night his entire life and, while this behavior doesn't become medically concerning until the age of about seven,[4] his father had little tolerance for it. Following every instance of bed-wetting, which was likely multiple times per week if not every night, the boy's father would make him hang his soiled sheets out his bedroom window to "shame him into bladder control."[2] The boy and his brother both claimed that their father would occasionally hang the boy out the window by his ankles when he was "really bad,"[1] and his niece later said, based on hearsay from her mother, that one time after he had peed his pants, the boy's father beat him in the head "real bad with a toy wooden airplane."[5] However, the boy later denied that and any other claim of physical abuse by his father.[2]

Although the boy was a genius with an IQ of 145, he struggled in school and failed the second grade, almost failing for a second time before his father stepped in with a rigorous tutoring curriculum that "forced him to learn."[2] Beyond academic struggles, the boy had a tough time socially and was bullied because of the shape of his head. His brother Terry said his oddly shaped head was due to the boy falling out of a tree when he was younger and landing on his head, also noting that his personality was never the same afterward.

The boy spent his spare time during middle school participating in Boy Scouts, working summer jobs, dating a bit, and reading. His two main interests were business and the military and "he devoured the financial sections of newspapers like other kids did comics."[1] His dream was twofold: 1) Become a millionaire, and 2) Attend West Point. In eighth grade he began wearing oversize military fatigues everywhere he went, ensuring that everyone he ran into knew exactly what his ambitions were.[1]

After quitting school in ninth grade, the teenager's father persuaded him to join a military academy so he could continue his studies in a more structured environment. He attended school here for the next two years before quitting again and returning home to his public high school. While the military school provided the structure he needed, it did nothing for his social skills and he continued to struggle socially when he returned home. He kept to himself, primarily engaging in activities such as reading and daydreaming rather than the activities of typical boys his age such as sports, clubs, and interpersonal relationships. At age 17, he quit school again and decided to join the army.[2]

After bootcamp, the teenager asked to be sent to the military police school but was turned down due to his age. He requested several other positions but was turned down again and again until finally he was offered a position as a medic. He graduated from training in Texas with excellent grades and became a well-regarded hospital corpsman who made more money than he ever had in his life. He decided to put all of his financial knowledge to work and became a "loan shark," hoarding his paychecks and loaning the money with interest to soldiers. Unfortunately, the Army sent the teenager to a new station in Germany before he was able to collect on his loans, so he lost nearly $5000.[1]

A few months after arriving in Germany and passing his high school equivalency exams with flying colors, he started experiencing symptoms such as vertigo, nausea, headaches, and blurred vision in one of his eyes. He was given a diagnosis of the stomach flu and the neurologist also noticed symptoms of mental illness such as "seizure-like behaviors that were thought to be hallucinatory and delusional."[2] He was prescribed an antipsychotic medication typical for patients with schizophrenia. Shortly thereafter, he was transferred to a hospital in Philadelphia, diagnosed with Schizoid Personality Disorder, and honorably discharged from the Army.[2]

CHAPTER 31

After the Army, the young man pursued a career in nursing. He became certified after completing a year of training, and also enrolled in the local university to earn credits in a variety of areas. He got a job at the university hospital but was fired after about four months due to chronic attendance issues accompanied by inappropriate and unprofessional interactions with patients. Finally, he got a job at a mental institution and was able to stick it out and find success.[1]

One of the young man's tasks at the mental institution was to drive his patients to and from excursions in the neighborhood. While doing so, he discovered that he could use his charm and authority and take these mentally challenged women to his home to have sex with them. Because they could not give informed consent due to limited intellectual capacity, the young man manipulated the situation for his own gain. His sole friends during this time were mentally handicapped men, who he could dominate, and women, who he could sleep with. His first documented relationship was with a woman named Lynn who had an intellectual disability; he also attempted to seduce her grown daughter, although there is no evidence as to whether he was successful. The young man and Lynn had a child, but again, there is no wellsourced documentation in mainstream coverage or public records about her fate. His longest relationship of 10 years was with a black woman named Dorothy who "suffered from chronic mental illness and a severe intellectual disability."[1]

Between 1962 and 1987, the man was in and out of mental institutions a documented 21 times and tried to commit suicide 13 times. His multiple suicide attempts were made using increasingly extreme methods. These included intentionally driving his motorcycle head-on into a truck, breaking a light bulb and swallowing the glass, overdosing on prescribed medications, and attempting to induce gangrene by tightly wrapping a cord around his big toe to cut off circulation. After each of these instances, the man 's diagnosis was confirmed: schizophrenia and anxiety.[2]

In 1971, the man had a psychotic episode where God commanded him to start a church for the mentally and physically handicapped that he later called the "Special Olympics of Churches."[1] He recruited five of his friends, named himself bishop, started the United Church of the Ministers of God[1]... and opened an investment account with Merryl Lynch.[2] Over time, the church became financially successful, largely due to the man's investment acumen. An initial $1,500 grew into a portfolio valued at approximately $545,000, and even his broker later described him as an astute investor. The church's constitution outlined how these funds were to be used, ostensibly for religious and administrative purposes such as property, education, utilities, and transportation. As the church accumulated wealth, its legitimacy increasingly came under scrutiny, with some institutions viewing it as a sophisticated tax-avoidance scheme, while others regarded it as a genuine humanitarian and religious organization.[2]

Despite these disputes, the church functioned in ways that appeared authentic to many observers. The man regularly held services, transported congregants, taught hymns to members who could not read, preached sermons, and organized group meals and outings. Witnesses described active worship gatherings and consistent participation, which challenged claims that the church was merely a financial front. By the mid-1980s, roughly fifteen years after its founding, the church was thriving both organizationally and financially.[2]

In June of 1977[1], while he was still with Dorothy, the man began a relationship with another intellectually disabled black woman named Anjeanette who had an IQ of 45 and was unable to read or write. He moved Anjeanette into his house with Dorothy and Anjeanette soon became pregnant, although the baby girl was put into foster care as soon as she was born due to her mother's disabilities.[2] The man was crushed and furious that the baby was taken away, so he devised a plan that would bring his fantasies to a whole new level.[1] He drove with Anjeanette to the mental institution that was housing her sister, Alberta, who had an IQ of 30.[2] There, the two signed Alberta out for a "home visit" and brought her back home to live with them. Once at home, he imprisoned Alberta in his basement for approximately ten days, during which time he repeatedly raped and sodomized her. During this period, he expressed delusional beliefs about impregnating her in order to father another child, operating under the distorted conviction that doing so would prevent authorities from removing the child from his custody.[1]

The man's horrific crime was discovered when a woman from the mental institution came by the house to see where Alberta was. The man denied knowing where she was, saying he put her on a bus back to the institution. The woman left reluctantly, but returned the next day with police officers. The officers searched the building and found Alberta cowering in the corner of the unfinished basement. Alberta was taken to the hospital and given tests, where irrefutable proof of her rape and sexual assault was found. The man was arrested and charged with "kidnapping, rape, false imprisonment, unlawful restraint, involuntary deviate sexual intercourse, interfering with the custody of a committed person, and recklessly endangering another person."[2]

Unfortunately, due to Alberta's intellectual limitations, she was deemed unfit to testify, resulting in the felony charges being dropped and the man being sentenced only on the remaining misdemeanor offenses.[2] In November 1978, the man was sentenced to seven years in prison but served just under four and a half years, spending the majority of that time in secure mental health units rather than the general prison population. He was released on parole in April 1983.[1]

When he was released, he was unable to locate Anjeanette and began to develop a fixed belief that he was entitled to a wife and a family. This sense of entitlement appeared to be rooted in resentment and distorted thinking, reflecting a growing expectation that society should provide him with the relationships and domestic life he believed he had been denied.[3]

CHAPTER 32

Finally out of prison, the man returned to his previous ways, befriending local mentally challenged individuals and getting his church up and going again. Still, though, his life needed a wife and children to be complete. In 1983, the man used a matrimonial service and began writing letters to a 22-year-old Filipino woman named Betty who, after two years, he finally convinced to move to the United States in October of 1985.[1] Betty's parents had urged her not to go and were not happy about her decision, but after two years of weekly letters, she thought she was in love. Despite being shocked at how much older he looked in person than in the pictures he had sent, Betty was overjoyed to finally be in her arms once she landed and they promptly got married. The first week of their relationship was the stuff of romance novels. The man treated Betty like a princess, kissing her in public, calling her "honey," and talking to her about what their future children would be like.[2] The return home from their honeymoon was the stuff of nightmares.

The man had expected her to be submissive and helpless, as the stereotype of a Filipino woman in the United States said she should be; later on in a letter he said he falsely believed "that oriental women would be the greatest wives ever in existence."[1] This, however, was not the case with Betty. Immediately upon their homecoming, he began raping and beating her and forcing her to have sex with other women.

Instead of submitting to this violent behavior like he had expected of her ("This is normal in America"[2]), Betty fled after just a few months. While he was arrested and charged with assault and rape, the charges were dropped[1] because Betty failed to show up to the hearing.[2]

On September 15th, Betty gave birth to the man's son and named him Jesse John. She told him about it via postcard and refused both reconciliation and divorce but both she and the court expected him to financially support her and their son. This led to a series of contentious court proceedings focused on his failure to meet spousal and child support obligations, during which his financial disclosures were repeatedly questioned. The court expressed concern about inconsistencies in his statements, uncertainty regarding the true extent of his assets, and whether his funds were personal or tied to the church, ultimately determining that further hearings and a comprehensive mental health evaluation were necessary before the matter could be resolved.[1]

Meanwhile, the man was in the midst of fulfilling his destiny– or so he thought. Society owed him a family but wasn't owning up, so he decided to create his own. His plan was to enslave ten black girls so he could impregnate them, birth mixed babies, and create the "perfect race." In this new society, white people would always mate with black people, and tall people would always mate with short people. Ultimately, this would serve the greater good and improve the world as a whole.[4]

On Thanksgiving Day 1986, the man, now 43-years-old, launched his plan. He drove through the city searching for a woman on the street and eventually encountered Josefina Rivera, a mixed-race woman with a Puerto Rican father and a Black mother. She had recently argued with her boyfriend, left to work, and was close to giving up for the night when he pulled alongside her. She needed the money. He offered her $20 to get into his car and go back to his house, and she agreed, giving him the name "Nicole," a name she commonly used with clients. At first, she was struck by his car, which appeared new and well kept, unaware it had been purchased only nine days earlier.[2]

That initial impression quickly faded. Under better lighting, she noticed his clothing was old and cheap and that he smelled unclean. Before taking her to his home, he stopped at McDonald's, where he bought himself a coffee but did not offer her anything. After their pitstop, they headed to the man's home– a small house in a poor neighborhood with a chain link fence and a front yard littered with trash.[2]

Once inside, the two went to the man's bedroom, where he paid his hooker and they had sex. Afterward, as she was getting dressed and getting ready to leave, she felt a strong grip around her neck, getting tighter and tighter. When he finally let go and she fell to the ground, she realized he had put handcuffs around her wrists. He forced her down the stairs and into the cold, damp, concrete-floored basement room where she would remain a prisoner for the next four months.[2]

Josefina may have felt like she was in a prison, but the man didn't look at it that way. He spoke to her at length about his desire to have a large family, framing himself as someone whose plans had repeatedly been taken from him. He claimed to have fathered four children with four different women, all of whom were no longer in his life due to the actions of the mothers or state authorities. He expressed particular resentment over his failed relationship with Anjeanette, with whom he had a daughter who was immediately placed into foster care, and he described his subsequent imprisonment following her and her sister falsely accusing him of rape. Presenting himself as wronged by the legal system, he told Josefina that society owed him a wife and a family, outlining a plan to keep multiple women captive, impregnate them, and raise the children together as what he described as a single, happy family.[2]

After sharing his plans with Josefina, he raped her and then went back upstairs, leaving her alone. Taking advantage of her solitude, she found a way to open the downstairs window, stuck her head out of it, and started screaming for help. A few minutes into her failed escape attempt, the man came running around the front of the house, shoved her head back through the window, then ran back inside and dragged her into a pit he had been digging in the floor of the basement. He beat her brutally with a stick and then pulled a piece of plywood over the hole and stuck bags of dirt over the top so she couldn't get out. Twenty-seven hours later, he let her out.

His family had been established, and it would only get worse from here.

CHAPTER 33

Over the next four months, Gary Heidnik would go on to rape and imprison six women and kill two of them. His anger at having lost his first wife and child and subsequent belief that society "owed" him a family lead him to abduct, torture, rape, and kill his victims in a hell-like dungeon.

Notably, Heidnik denied being a serial killer, claiming, "I am by no means a serial killer. Those two deaths were purely accidental. There was no willful intent or premeditation on my part to kill anyone."[1] He framed his actions as an attempt to create a self-contained "family" or social group in which he held absolute control. He described this group as one designed to meet his emotional and psychological needs, ensuring constant access to companionship, validation, and a sense of belonging, while eliminating the possibility of rejection or abandonment by those within it.[1]

One week after kidnapping Josefina, Heidnik brought his second prisoner, Sandra Lindsay, down to the basement. Sandra, another black woman, differed from Josefina in that she had known Heidnik for several years prior to her captivity and she had graduated from the special education program in high school. Her boyfriend, Tony, was Heidnik's closest friend, and Sandra had previously lived in one of the apartments Heidnik owned and rented. The three were involved in an unconventional relationship in which both men engaged in sexual relationships with her. At one point, Sandra became pregnant with Heidnik's child but chose to terminate the pregnancy. Heidnik reacted angrily, condemning abortion as immoral, and later offered her money to carry his child. When she refused, he reportedly told her that she would have his baby regardless of her wishes. The next thing she knew, she was in Heidnik's cellar with Josefina.[2]

To call Heidnik's form of torture "cruel and unusual" would be to grossly underrepresent it. He raped them on a daily basis, focusing not on his own sexual gratification but on impregnating them. Afterward, he seemed to enjoy their presence and would spend time chatting to them as though they were old friends and not victims that he had just viciously raped. When they "misbehaved," Heidnik would punish them by putting them in the hole he'd dug, covering it with a board and bags of sand, and only feeding them bread and water, if anything, for the next day or two. He also used "stretch punishment" by handcuffing one wrist to an overhead pipe and making them stand there with one arm above their head for hours on end.[2]

Victim number three was 19-year-old Lisa Thomas, who was abducted just two days before Christmas. His fourth was 23-year-old Deborah Dudley on January 2, 1987. After adding these two to his harem, his need for dominance and control somehow turned up a notch. On top of the daily rapings, he forced the girls to have sex with each other and continued to give them only enough food to keep from starving, occasionally treating them by giving them an extra helping of dog food. Heidnik's fifth victim was 18-year-old Jaqueline Askins on January 18th; his sixth was 24-year-old Agnes Adams on March 23, 1987.[1]

In addition to the obvious physical trauma Heidnik inflicted on his victims, the psychological damage was profound and deliberately engineered. As more women were confined in the basement, a rigid social structure emerged, shaped by Heidnik's manipulation rather than by choice. Josefina gradually gained a position of relative favor. Over time, she appeared to receive fewer punishments, and other captives later noted that she was rarely subjected to the physical abuse routinely inflicted on the rest. Despite very much still being his prisoner and being terrified of him, she became his go-to for helping him punish others or cover up his "mishaps."[2]

Heidnik asserted authority by forcing the women into roles that guaranteed conflict and fear. When he left them unattended, he assigned one victim temporary authority and later interrogated her about the others' behavior. Any response led to harm: reporting misconduct resulted in punishment for the group, while denying it resulted in punishment for the spokesperson. He further coerced the women into harming one another, escalating or reversing roles when he felt the violence was insufficient. This system fractured any sense of safety or unity, compelling the victims to participate in their own oppression and intensifying the psychological torment alongside the physical abuse.[2]

Several weeks into captivity when Sandra attempted to escape and failed, she was cuffed to the pipe for 48 hours straight. After being freed from the handcuffs, Sandra was barely conscious and, when she could keep her eyes open, couldn't stop vomiting. Heidnik was delighted and attributed this to her being pregnant, obviously. When she collapsed, though, he assumed she was faking it, became furious, and threw her into the pit. When he returned later, Sandra was dead.[1] After forcing Josefina to help him carry the body upstairs, Heidnik used a power saw to dismember it and later fed the body parts to the other victims, mixing them with rice and dog food and freezing what remained.[1]

By the time he had added what would be his final victim, Agnes, to the mix, he had once again upped his terror. He severely handicapped the original four (minus Josefina) by puncturing their eardrums with a screwdriver so they couldn't hear when he came or went from the house. He also started shocking them using a combination of electric cords and metal handcuffs. On March 18, 1987, Heidnik forced Josefina to fill the pit with water, then had the women stand in the water and sent an electric current through it. Electrifying the water like this would likely have caused severe pain, violent muscle contractions, loss of motor control, and a risk of cardiac or respiratory failure. All of the women screamed in pain but in Deborah's case, the effect was lethal. She died almost instantly due to the wire directly touching the chains around her ankles.[1]

The next day, after leaving the body in a freezer overnight, Heidnik and Josefina disposed of it in a nearby forest. Five days later, on March 24, 1987, Josefina escaped and told the police everything that had happened. Heidnik was arrested on March 25th and the girls were rescued.

The surviving victims of Gary Heidnik carried the consequences of his crimes long after the basement was uncovered. In the immediate aftermath, some of the women blamed Josefina Rivera for her perceived cooperation with Heidnik and even believed she should have been prosecuted alongside him. Due to the fact that Rivera is the one who rescued them all, though, she was not convicted. Years later, Jaqueline Askins and Rivera met again and confronted the pain and blame that had divided them, ultimately reaching a fragile understanding that allowed both women to move forward, if not healed, then no longer alone in what they had survived. While Rivera eventually rebuilt her life, raising children and maintaining steady work, she continued to struggle with panic attacks and lasting psychological scars. Askins also raised her sons while managing anxiety and flashbacks tied to her imprisonment. Lisa Thomas and Agnes Adams never fully recovered and lived with severe mental health and substance use issues for the rest of their lives. Several of the victims and family members attended Heidnik's execution in 1999, though many later said it brought little closure. In the end, Heidnik's death closed a case, but the survivors were left to carry the real sentence for the rest of their lives.[3]

CHAPTER 34

Gary Heidnik's behavior reflected a complex mix of intelligence, manipulation, and distorted thinking. Early experiences with strict discipline, instability, and emotional neglect helped shape his need for control and his sense of entitlement. As an adult, these patterns developed into a rigid belief system that justified extreme measures to create a "family" that would meet his needs. Examining Heidnik's psychology involves looking at both his actions and the thought processes behind them, including the obsessions, resentments, and delusions that guided his behavior.

In the competency proceedings meant to determine if Heidnik was competent to stand trial, several psychiatrists diagnosed him with paranoid schizophrenia, noting that his fixed beliefs and distorted thinking affected his perception of reality and could interfere with understanding legal proceedings or working with counsel. A psychiatrist for the prosecution, however, testified that Heidnik did not show signs of schizophrenia or delusions at the time of evaluation and was mentally competent. The district court, however, rejected the prosecution's core conclusions, finding Heidnik to be delusional and suffering from paranoid schizophrenia.[1]

Heidnik's delusions were evident from day one. In 1971, he had a psychotic episode that prompted him to drive thousands of miles to the Pacific Ocean, where he then claimed to have been commanded by God to start a church for the mentally challenged. In letters he wrote from prison after his conviction, he claimed his marriage to Anjeanette had been doomed from the start because the racists wanted to keep them apart. He said they hated that he, a white man, had married a black woman and were trying to have babies, so they lied and framed him for rape and had him sent to prison.[2]

He also continued insisting he was not a serial killer, saying both deaths that occurred in his basement were accidental and even going as far as to say he had nothing to do with them. In regards to Sandra's death, he claimed he only made her stand with her arm above her head for an hour and a half and "How the hell can standing up for an hour and a half be fatal?"[2] As for Deborah, Heidnik claims he was shocked through the water many times as a child and he never died. He also shifted the blame to Josefina, saying she was the one who touched the electrical current to Deborah's chains, but still maintaining it was an accidental death and to call it murder is a "miscarriage of terminology since there was no intent to kill." Ultimately, he showed no empathy for his victims, offering no remorse or acknowledgment of the tragedy of their deaths. Instead, he expressed anger over what he saw as a false conviction and claimed to have endured far more ("50 times more") suffering than those he harmed.[2]

Let's take a deeper look at what it means to have schizophrenia. Schizophrenia is characterized by a range of symptoms that affect thinking, perception, behavior, and emotions. Individuals may experience persistent delusions, holding fixed false beliefs despite evidence to the contrary, and hallucinations, perceiving things that are not present. They may feel that their thoughts, actions, or feelings are controlled or influenced by external forces, or that their thoughts are being broadcast to others. Disorganized thinking often appears as jumbled or irrelevant speech, while highly disorganized behavior can be bizarre, purposeless, or accompanied by inappropriate emotional responses that disrupt daily functioning. Negative symptoms include limited speech, restricted emotions, lack of interest or pleasure, and social withdrawal. Additionally, some individuals may show extreme agitation, slowed movements, or maintain unusual postures.[3]

It's impossible to know if Heidnik suffered from hallucinations besides seeing God on the Pacific Ocean and being told to start a church, but he obviously suffered from "persistent delusions." Despite that, his IQ goes against the stereotype that people with schizophrenia are "impaired" across all areas. However, his high intelligence could have helped him hide or "mask" the disorder in his earlier years, and the confidence he undoubtedly had in his ideas likely made others question themselves rather than Heidnik himself.

Heidnik's primary delusion was believing that because he couldn't naturally fit into any societal social circles, he needed to create his own that was forced to accept him no matter what.

"A unique way of looking at what I did in my disturbed state of mind was to create my own social group or family if you wish. It was a social group in which I was the only male, the only economic provider, the patriarch so to speak, and which was available to me 24 hours a day. Since I couldn't achieve a sense of belonging to any of the other existing social groups in American society, I endeavored to create my own social group. One that had to accept me and couldn't abandon me and had to provide the things I needed, love, bonding, children, companionship, etc. For instance, any time I felt a need to talk they were there. Where could they go? They had to listen."[2]

Gary Heidnik's behaviors cannot be excused by his mental capacities or lack thereof. A mental diagnosis helps us see behind the curtain, but it does not provide allowances for someone acting the way he did, especially when it involves kidnapping, rape, and murder. While mental illness may help explain aspects of his thinking, it does not erase intent, planning, or repeated choices to inflict harm. Heidnik demonstrated awareness of his actions, took steps to conceal them, and exercised control over his victims, all of which point to responsibility rather than incapacity. Understanding his psychological profile adds context, but it should never dilute accountability or shift focus away from the suffering he deliberately caused.

PART 8

DADDY'S LITTLE GIRL

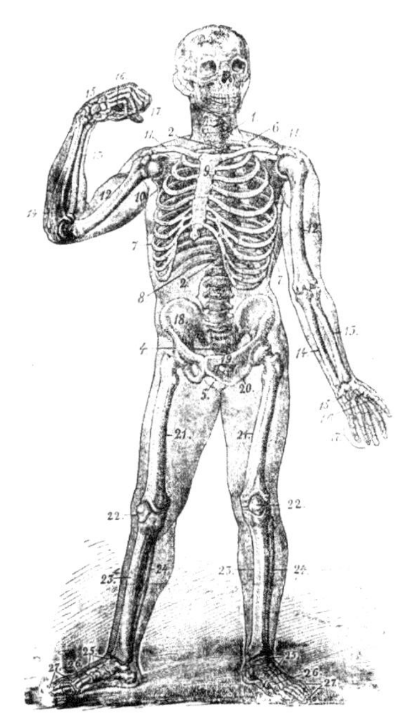

CHAPTER 35

It's a beautiful day outside, but the little girl has no way of knowing that. She's been inside for days, doing chores and helping her mother make sure the house shines for her father's return. She doesn't leave the house for school, yard work, or even to play with friends. If she's honest, she's excited but nervous about her father's return. The way he treats her is different from how he treats the rest of her siblings. He tells her she's special and she can't tell anyone what they do together. She understands it's fatherly love, but she isn't sure why she has to keep it secret.

Twenty-three years before our antagonist was born, her parents, Daisy and Bill, tied the knot at ages 21 and 23. Their first year of marriage was happy enough, featuring homeownership and a new baby. They were both thankful to be leaving their parents and starting their own families, as neither set of parents knew how to show them love in the way they deserved. Bill's father had told him repeatedly as he grew up that he was never wanted and his mother seemed to have an obsessive need to keep the house so clean, Bill didn't feel like he was allowed to be a kid. However, his mother spoiled him and babied him to make up for the lack of love from his father, who would do things like force him to sleep outside in the shed if he came home too late as a teenager. Daisy's mother, on the other hand, had sclerosis of the liver, which is often due to alcoholism. It was rumored that as a child Daisy was sent to live in a children's home for a time after mysterious burns were found all over her body. Needless to say, both Bill and Daisy were thankful to be paving their own way.[1]

In 1943, Bill was called to the war as a radio mechanic in the Navy. Over the next 9 years, Bill was rarely home and Daisy played the role of primary caregiver to her children. With Daisy in charge, life was simple, free of unnecessary burdens such as friendships, and very, very clean. Their neighbors remember them being beautiful, well-fed, and well-dressed, but they were rarely allowed outside. Although Bill was away at sea much of the time, he seemed to have a sort of control over Daisy, as she was "overly concerned with the hygiene and the state of the house."[1] By 1951, Daisy was showing signs of neurosis and severe anxiety, and started sinking into a deep depression. Her neighbors called her "disturbed" and said they frequently heard her yelling at her children.[1]

In 1952, Bill left the Navy to return home and care for his sick wife and their children. That same year, the couple got pregnant again and gave birth to their fourth child– their first boy. 1953 found Daisy's mental health sinking to depths no one could have imagined. She developed agoraphobia and refused to even open the door to the outside; she likely had postpartum depression, although very little was known about it at the time so it went undiagnosed. What her psychiatrist did end up prescribing was a course of electric shock treatment (ECT), which both Daisy and Bill readily agreed to.[1]

Immediately and coincidentally, Daisy fell pregnant again. This time, with a little girl. Despite Daisy's pregnancy, her husband and doctor insisted that she continue the electric shock treatment until the entire prescribed course was finished. As the child grew silently in her mother's womb,

Daisy endured repeated rounds of ECT, each shock triggering violent convulsions, with the final treatment administered just days before she gave birth.[1]

On November 29, 1953, the girl was born.

As an infant, the girl repeatedly rocked and bashed her head for long periods, both in her baby carriage and at night, to the point that it disturbed her siblings, yet she was still described as a "good baby" because she rarely cried. Her lack of crying continued as she grew older, alongside a tendency to rock her head for long periods and enter trance-like, vacant states in which she appeared withdrawn from the world around her.[1]

As the girl grew, she struggled to grasp basic academic concepts and frustrated anyone who tried to teach her, because she just didn't get it. She flew under the radar at school and her peers barely noticed her presence; her teachers later said she was polite, steady, and sensible. She talked in a baby-like voice, never raised her hand in class, and sucked her thumb until she was far too old to be sucking her thumb.[1]

At home, the girl had what looked like a typical childhood to everyone inside the house and no one outside the house. Her father, Bill, who no one knew was a diagnosed paranoid schizophrenic until after his death, was extremely abusive to his wife and all seven of the children the two ended up having. He had developed obsessive-compulsive disorder and demanded that there not be even a speck of dust anywhere, lest he fly into a fit of disproportionate rage and take it out on whoever was the closest. When Bill was home, he used his fists to communicate his feelings, although his wife told him to make sure not to leave bruises anywhere that couldn't be hidden by kids' clothes. When he was away, he was sure his wife was cheating on him and told the vendors in town not to serve her if she came around. Bill demanded obedience simply because he believed his authority was absolute. Whether Daisy complied or not made little difference, as violence followed both defiance and submission.[1]

As expected, the seven kids lived in fear of their violent father. If his rules went unfollowed, chaos would follow. On one occasion, Bill spoiled all the food they had in the house by pouring salt in it so his family would have nothing to eat. On another, the kids didn't wake up on time and Bill poured a bucket of ice water over them. When Daisy was on the front porch talking to a neighbor, Bill punched her in the face and dragged her inside by the hair while the neighbors watched in shock. He was particularly threatened by Andy, his eldest son, who he saw as competition and a threat to his masculinity. Later, Andy said that at one point his father beat him so badly that if his mother hadn't stepped in, his father would have killed him. Of course, this fed into Bill's delusion that the world was against him and he promptly attacked Daisy. As a teenager, Andy started spending more and more time at his girlfriend's house and was shocked that she and her siblings could talk and laugh at the dinner table, and watch a movie with their dad without fear of a beating.[1]

The girl may have been slow to learn in school, but she was a quick study when it came to appeasing her father. She knew how to stay out of his way so she could avoid the physical abuse, and how to manipulate him into feeling sorry for her so he would let her off. It was around this time that Bill started sexually assaulting the girl, who had learned that all she had to do was satisfy her father and she would avoid the physical abuse her siblings and mother received. Others didn't take the abuse so easily; when he tried to assault her 15-year-old sister, Patricia, she resisted and he threw her down the stairs. Bill was so enamored by young people, particularly young girls, that he started a youth club with a friend. Shortly after, his family picked up and moved in the middle of the night. It was rumored that social services had picked up on the fact that Bill was using the club as a way to sexually abuse young girls in the community.[1]

Years later, while in prison, the girl wrote a letter to a friend saying, "My parents were sick people who should never have had children in the first place. They were control freaks and at their hands we suffered mental, physical and sexual abuse … No one cared for us EVER!"[1]

CHAPTER 36

The girl was bullied and beat up by peers throughout her entire childhood, but she stopped letting it happen once she hit her teenage years. She'd gained considerable weight and used her weight to put a stop to the bullying, gaining the reputation of being "hard" and taking revenge on those who used to beat her up. She also started standing up to her dad when he would physically abuse her two younger siblings, becoming their protector from the age of just 13.[1]

Also at age 13, the teenager started practicing the sexual exploits she had learned from her father on her two younger brothers, Graham and Gordon, who were nine and six at the time. She began regularly sexually assaulting them by using her hand to sexually stimulate them. She also regularly paraded naked around the house in front of her brothers and her father, apparently unbothered by their gazes. Once she lost interest in sexual activity with her brothers and father, she started seeking out other boys in the town, inviting them to her home when her parents were away or visiting theirs, and encouraging them to touch her inappropriately.[1]

By 15, she tried to have sex with her brother-in-law, was later picked up by the cops for "street walking," and was exchanging sex with men twice her age for a place to sleep. By 16, she was having sex with her then 12-year-old brother, Graham, continuing this until she left home.[1]

Around 1968, Daisy had had enough of the physical abuse and left her husband, taking her three youngest kids with her and moving in with her 18-year-old daughter, Glenys. According to a later tale by the teenager, one day she came home to Glenys' house to find her mother and brothers had packed up and moved out. She felt betrayed and scared and decided to move back in with her father, from whom she had not experienced the same physical abuse that the rest of the family had received. Upon moving home, the teenager went back to her old ways of keeping her father happy by giving him everything he asked for. This incestuous relationship between father and daughter lasted until Bill died, and it is also believed that she engaged in a similar relationship with her grandfather.[1]

In late summer 1969, the teenager met Fred– the man who was to become her future husband and partner in literal crime.

Fred was a troubled boy who left school at 14, barely able to read or write, and grew up in a cramped home where he and his six siblings shared just two bedrooms. His childhood was marked by severe abuse, and these acts became the only form of attention or affection he ever knew. His father regularly beat and sexually assaulted his wife and daughters, raped other young girls, and forced his sons to watch the violence. In addition to this, he taught Fred to have sex with animals, showing him exactly how it was done.[1]

Fred was also raped by his mother, who doted on and babied her 12-year-old son from the time he was born. By the time he was 16 years old in 1957, he had learned how to impress the ladies in town and started regularly having sex, which made his 33-year-old mother jealous. In the summer of 1957, Fred left home in the middle of the night to work and create a life of his own. He came home in 1960 and started sleeping with his mother again. He also started sleeping with his 13-year-old sister, getting her pregnant and was consequently arrested. At the trial, his mother provided evidence for his defense and his pregnant sister refused to name the father of her baby, so the case was dismissed. Afterward, he celebrated by going home and raping the first girl he met. Notably, Fred never denied having sex with his sister, he was just nonplussed that he had gotten in trouble for something that was perfectly normal in the family he grew up in.[1]

Wedding bells didn't quite ring when 28-year-old Fred met the 15-year-old. They were both at a bus stop and he asked her out twice to no avail. When she got on the bus to go home, he followed her, sat next to her, and the two proceeded to get to know each other for the next six or so miles. By the time they had arrived at the teenager's bus stop, he asked again and was delighted that she said "yes."[1]

The two dated in secret for a time, going to pubs on the other side of town where the teenager's father wouldn't catch wind of their relationship. When the teenager turned down a beautiful dress and coat Fred had gifted her due to not wanting her father to find out, he eagerly told her he'd keep her clothes at his house and she could come by anytime she wanted. Fred was also excited to introduce the teenager to his daughters, who he had been sexually abusing their whole lives and whose mother he had beaten so often that she finally ran off. The teenager loved the children and began regularly babysitting them, eventually quitting her job and becoming a full-time nanny, soon-to-be stepmother, for them. When the teenager wasn't able to watch the kids, Fred would entice local schoolgirls to watch them and would pay them with sex.[1]

When the teenager finally decided she was done hiding her lover and she wanted her parents to meet him, they were less than impressed and told her to never see that "filthy gypsy" again. Obviously, the teenager didn't listen. By this time Fred was paying her a small amount for watching his girls and so her parents wouldn't become suspicious that she was no longer bringing money home. Upon Fred's arrival home every night, she would have sex with him and then run home to her parent's house where she would sexually assault her brothers before going to bed.[1]

CHAPTER 37

Life with Fred wasn't what the teenager expected. Their sex life was best when Fred was tied up and beaten or when he was watching her have sex with someone else. He consistently made references to his ex-wife and her sexual antics, manipulating the teenager into thinking she needed to be more like the ex-wife to be loved. His ex was a prostitute so soon enough, the teenager jumped into the sex-work scene with both feet.

When Bill found out that his daughter had quit her job and was working as a sex worker instead, he became enraged and called child services, getting her sent to a home for troubled teenagers. This home had strict rules about where she could go and whom she could see, meaning she wasn't allowed to see Fred. As every rebellious teenager does, she figured out a way to see her lover for small amounts of time and also began writing him letters. During this time apart, Fred got back with his ex-wife and it infuriated the teenager to know that the ex-wife could sneak in any chance she got.[1]

Shortly after the teenager got out of the home and Fred was released from a 30-day stint in jail for failure to pay fines and possession of a stolen tax disc, she decided to get rid of the ex-wife for good by having Fred's baby. As luck would have it, they got pregnant almost immediately. While the couple celebrated, the teenager's parents did the exact opposite when they found out. Daisy refused to talk to her and Bill beat her and then called social services again, getting her sent to another home to try and bring her to her senses. While she stayed there, Bill arranged for the teenager to have an abortion, which she agreed to and then ran away with Fred instead.[1]

Fred and the teenager finally found a house to live in in the summer of 1970. The two of them moved in with Fred's daughters, Charmaine (age 8) and Anne-Marie (age 6), and their newest baby girl, Heather, born in October 1970. Life was decent for a while. Fred had multiple jobs to support the family while the teenager worked in the home, caring for the home and the girls. However, Fred had a penchant for stealing things and he soon got caught, earning himself nine months in prison.[1]

This meant that now the 16-year-old was solely responsible for two little girls who weren't biologically hers, and one infant that was increasingly fussy. Anne-Marie lived to please and was timid and quiet, much like how the teenager was as a child. Charmaine, on the other hand, was angry and argumentative, telling the teenager every chance she got that she wasn't her mom and couldn't tell her what to do.[1]

This wasn't the life Fred had promised her.

Coping as best as she could, the teenager started following her own mother and father's examples when it came to child-rearing. Since Fred had given her full control of disciplining the girls while he was in prison, the teenager took it upon herself to make sure they knew who was in charge. She insisted that the girls did all the housework and if anything was not up to her impossible standard, she would take to beating them without whatever object was nearest. She also refused to let the girls go out to play or have friends other than their upstairs neighbor, Tracy. This, she discovered, gave her a feeling of power that she had never had before.[1]

As the months went by, the teenager upped her abuse, experimenting with increasingly sadistic tactics. On one occasion, she broke a ceramic bowl over Anne-Marie's head, resulting in the child being rushed to the ER and needing stitches. On another occasion, their friend Tracy came in the front door unannounced to see Charmaine standing on a chair with her hands tied behind her back and her stepmother seconds away from beating her with a spoon. The teenager also tortured the children while they were sleeping by stripping them of their clothes and tying them to their beds at night, refusing to allow them to make even a sound.[1]

All along, Charmaine refused to cry or complain, remaining defiantly against her soon-to-be stepmother. This angered the teenager because she didn't feel as though she had full control over the child, and her abuse against Charmaine became even worse. She began to confine her to the bedroom for the entire day, binding her hands behind her back and restraining her legs to the bed. She also regularly gagged both girls with strips of sheet so their neighbors couldn't hear them cry out when she beat them with a leather strap.[1]

Fred was no help. All he told her was not to leave bruises on the girls where they would show.[1]

Somewhere around early summer of 1971, the teenager committed her first murder by killing Charmaine. While no one knows exactly what happened, it is said to have occurred somewhere between May 7, 1971 and June 24, 1971, when the body could be hidden in the attic before Fred returned home from prison. Rumors later circulated that the teenager killed Charmaine during an episode of violence following prolonged abuse and confinement. Some accounts suggest the death may have been accidental, occurring during punishment or restraint, while others claim it was deliberate. No definitive cause of death was ever established since her body wasn't found for another 20 years, and the circumstances surrounding Charmaine's disappearance remain unresolved.[1]

After Fred's release from prison, Charmaine's body was taken upstairs and dismembered, drawing on skills he had learned years earlier while working in an abattoir. Some small bones were removed and kept as mementos, though it is unclear whether the girl was aware of this. Later that night, a grave was dug near the kitchen door, and the child's remains were buried there, possibly with Rose's assistance. Several years later, when a kitchen extension was built, the body was exhumed and reburied beneath the new structure, where it remained concealed for decades before finally being discovered.[1]

With Charmaine's death behind them, the teenager and Fred moved forward into married life, marking the beginning of what would become one of the most notorious serial killing partnerships on record.

CHAPTER 38

In the years that followed, Rose West became deeply involved in a long pattern of abuse and murder alongside her husband, Fred West. Together, they targeted young women and girls, holding them captive in their home, abusing them over time, and eventually killing them. Rose was not just present; she actively took part in the abuse and helped keep the victims under control. These crimes continued for years and were hidden in plain sight, later making Rose West one of the most infamous female killers in modern British history.

After murdering and burying Charmaine, Rose got spooked and ran home to her father, who hated having been left in the first place and sent her right back home to Fred. When Rose followed his instructions and left to go back to Fred, Bill ran after her saying he was kidding and she was allowed to come home. Unfortunately for them both, the deed was done and Rose returned to her lover and partner in crime.

Fred and Rose West were responsible for a series of at least 12 murders between the late 1960s and 1987, many of them committed together at their *25 Cromwell Street* home in Gloucester, later called the "House of Horrors." Their victims ranged from young women they lured or picked up to children known to them, and most were sexually abused, killed, and buried either in the cellar or garden of the house; skeletal remains were later uncovered during police investigations.

Fred and Rose's first known murder as a couple was Lynda Gough, who lived locally and had attended schools in the area her whole life. At the time of her murder she was working as a seamstress[3] and engaging in group sex with the couple. She was reported missing in April 1973 and her remains were found under the house the Wests lived in. Their second murder was Carole Ann Cooper, or "Caz." Caz had been on her way to spend the weekend with her grandmother when she was picked up as a hitchhiker by the Wests, taken to their house, and murdered.

This same trend can be seen nine more times with Lucy Partington, Therese Siegenthaler, Shirley Hubbard, Juanita Mott, Shirley Anne Robinson, Alison Chambers, and Heather West.

Lucy Partington was a 21-year-old college student from Gloucestershire who was intelligent, sociable, and well-liked by her classmates. Therese Siegenthaler, also 21, was a Swiss student studying secretarial studies in London and planning to travel to Ireland to visit a friend. Lynda Gough, around 21, was friendly and outgoing, while Carole Ann Cooper, 15, was a bright schoolgirl with a love of learning and a cheerful personality. Shirley Hubbard, 15, was quiet and polite, described by friends as considerate and kind. Juanita Mott, 18, was energetic and lively, known for her sense of humor and easy-going nature. Shirley Anne Robinson, 18, was responsible and independent, a lodger who had taken on work while living with the Wests. Alison Chambers, about 16, was a thoughtful young woman who had lived in a children's home and was preparing to start a new chapter in her life.[2,3]

Fred and Rose West's final known murder was their own 16-year-old daughter, Heather. Heather was known as rebellious, independent, and completely unafraid of her parents. She had just finished her GCSE examinations when she went missing after threatening to call the cops on her parents. She was buried under the patio and was the first of Fred and Rose's victims to be found.[3]

Rose West was arrested on April 20, 1994. While she maintained that she was innocent and a victim of her husband, she was charged with ten counts of murder while Fred was charged with twelve. Fred died by suicide before the trial date, but Rose was sentenced to life in prison without parole. As of 2026, she is still in prison.

CHAPTER 39

Rose West's childhood was ridiculously traumatic and it's no surprise that she did not escape unscathed. There is no publicly confirmed psychiatric diagnosis for Rose West in the academic or medical record, but the information we do have about her describe behaviors consistent with severe personality pathology, including manipulation, lack of empathy, and cruelty. These characteristics overlap with what clinicians describe in profiles of individuals with psychopathic traits, but without access to formal psychiatric records, it would be speculative and irresponsible to label her with a specific clinical diagnosis.

In addition to a high probability of antisocial personality disorder, Rose displayed plenty of sadistic traits. Anne-Marie once said of her adoptive mother, "Rose would have made a wonderful concentration camp guard… nothing would have pleased her more than to send many to their deaths."[1] Sadism refers to a pattern where a person experiences pleasure, satisfaction, or a sense of power from causing pain, fear, humiliation, or suffering in others. That suffering can be physical, emotional, or psychological. The key piece is that the other person's distress is not incidental. It is the point.[2] Growing up in a household with a sadistic father, Rose implemented what she learned from him and turned up the intensity even more, going from graduating from raping her brothers to murdering her boyfriend's daughter to eventually murdering her own flesh and blood... and showing no remorse or guilt. She enjoyed the feeling of control she had when she caused pain to others, and very likely murdered Charmaine because the girl wasn't showing pain or distress the way everyone else was.

One of the most interesting and controversial– albeit least violent– parts of Rose's childhood happened before she was even born: When her mother had electroconvulsive therapy from the day she became pregnant until the day before she gave birth. While there is a lot of internet commentary on this fact and armchair experts certain that they're right, there has been plenty of research on ECT in pregnancy and very little, if any, is negative.[5] What is more relevant, however, is that Daisy, Rose's mother, also experienced significant depression during her pregnancy, which is why she tried ECT. Studies on prenatal maternal depression suggest that children born to mothers with depression are at higher risk of later emotional or behavioral difficulties, particularly if they experience maltreatment or instability after birth. In other words, while ECT itself is unlikely to have caused direct harm, the combination of maternal mental illness and a stressful early environment could have influenced Rose's neurodevelopment and emotional regulation.[6]

In that same realm of Nature vs. Nurture, while it's likely she had some genetic disposition toward mental disorders from her mother's depression and her father's hidden diagnosis of paranoid schizophrenia, that alone wasn't the reason she turned into a sadistic serial rapist and murderer. "Nurture" clearly plays a very strong role in her psychosis and the environment and people she grew up around heavily influenced who she became.

The most consistent part of Rose's childhood was sexual abuse: Both the abuse she received and later the abuse she inflicted on others. Childhood sexual abuse is a severe adverse childhood experience with well-documented long-term consequences, including higher rates of adult mental health disorders, poorer psychological and physical health, and lower overall quality of life. While childhood sexual abuse does not determine future behavior, it is a significant risk factor that can distort development, relationships, and emotional regulation across the lifespan.[3]

In 1984, the CDC introduced the "Behavioral Risk Factor Surveillance System" (BRFSS) to better understand how certain behaviors impact quality of life. In a large sample of nearly 11,000 adults from the Texas BRFSS, just over 10% reported experiencing some form of childhood sexual abuse by someone at least five years older. The most commonly reported experiences were being touched sexually as a child, followed by being forced to touch another person sexually, and being forced to have sex. Rates were consistently higher for females than males across every category. Nearly 15% of women reported some form of childhood sexual abuse, compared to just over 5% of men. Women were more than three times as likely to report being sexually touched as children and more than twice as likely to report being forced to have sex.[3]

In the same study, childhood sexual assault by itself was linked to significantly worse adult health outcomes. Individuals who experienced sexual assault as a child had 51% higher odds of rating their general health as fair or poor, 46% higher odds of reporting more physically unhealthy days, 86% higher odds of more mentally unhealthy days, and 122% higher odds of experiencing greater activity limitations in a month.[3] In addition to this, a 1995 study found that of 91 sexual offenders who targeted children found that a majority had been sexually abused themselves as children. Additionally, about three-quarters of the offenders reported they would continue abusing children, highlighting a pattern of continuity in abusive behavior.[4] Unfortunately for Rose's victims, she fits into this pattern of the offended becoming the offender.

At the end of the day, Rose West was a deeply traumatized woman who committed horrific acts, not only against the ten people she murdered, but against their families and countless others she abused in different ways. Her traumatic history does not excuse her actions, but it does provide context for understanding how she may have come to commit such crimes. At the same time, her stepdaughter Anne-Marie, who experienced similar circumstances, went on to live an adulthood free from sexual abuse and criminal behavior. This contrast underscores an important truth: traumatic childhood experiences or a genetic predisposition toward mental health challenges do not determine destiny. Most children who endure adversity grow up to lead healthy, functional lives, and understanding risk factors is about identifying where support is needed, not assuming a dark fate is inevitable.

PART 9

A WEIRD LITTLE BASTARD

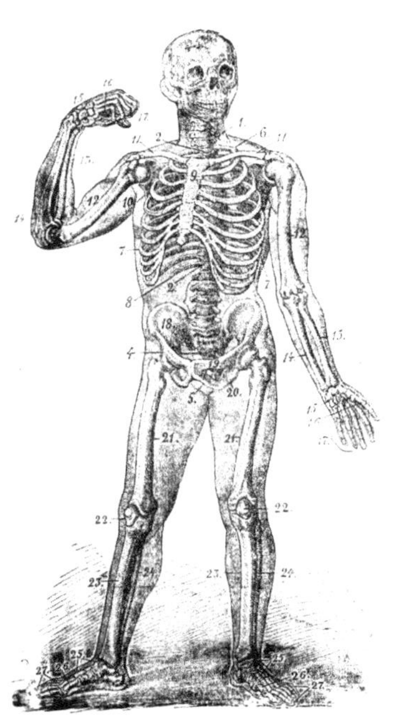

CHAPTER 40

On a gray upstate New York afternoon in the early 1950s, a small boy drifted along the edges of his neighborhood, lingering where he was neither invited nor missed. He was thin, socially awkward, and habitually alone, moving with the quiet detachment of a child who had learned that attention was inconsistent and rarely comforting. Inside his home, structure existed without warmth, discipline without connection. Outside, he wandered, watching more than participating, retreating inward when interaction felt risky. Nothing about the scene appeared extraordinary, and that ordinariness is precisely what makes it unsettling. No single moment foreshadowed what he would become, only a slow accumulation of isolation, resentment, and an inner world increasingly cut off from others.[1]

It was July 1943 and the subject of the newspaper article was Arthur's marriage to Thelma in February of that same year. The newspaper also noted that the couple had a three-month-old son named Harley. Just over one year later, in November of 1944, Arthur married Betty. There was never any mention of Thelma or Harley again; it was like the marriage had never happened.[1]

Arthur dropped out of school in 8th grade and then enlisted in the Marine Corps when Pearl Harbor was bombed. At one point while deployed in Japan, he was buried and almost suffocated if a friend hadn't remembered where he'd been right before the enemy shell went off. Another time, he and his outfit were cut off and had to live on rotting Japanese food that was full of maggots for several months.[1]

When Arthur met Betty, the latter was 18 years old and had quit school in 10th grade to work in a shoe factory. Her parents were of Mediterranean descent and raised her in that fashion, emphasizing obedience, family loyalty, and traditional gender roles, with limited encouragement for independence or prolonged education. This type of upbringing was not unusual for working-class families of the time and does not, on its own, suggest dysfunction or abuse.[1]

On June 6, 1945, Betty gave birth to their little boy at a Naval hospital in Maine. He was born two months premature, weighed only five pounds, and had to stay in the hospital with Betty for the next 20 days. The boy had brown hair and dark eyes. He hardly cried and his face remained blank most of the time, with a lack of affect. Betty breastfed the boy for two months and weaned him from the bottle by a year and a half. He spoke his first words at nine months, walked at 15 months, and spent most of his day in his crib due to the small apartment the family lived in. According to relatives, the boy was "a weird little bastard" as a toddler. He made weird noises, his facial expressions were lacking, and when he did cry one of his eyes always stayed dry. He was happy and well-loved, though, and that was all that mattered to Betty.[1]

The boy never really grew out of his oddities as he got older. In fact, they only seemed to increase. His peers said he didn't have any friends, but that didn't seem to bother him. He was still talking in "baby talk" while in Kindergarten, he had frequent nightmares and therefore wet the bed often, and he began running away from home starting in first grade. During one such instance, he was missing for hours and had the whole town scouring the area for him. Once he was bored with the mayhem, he crawled out from under the house where he'd been watching the chaos ensue. This type of attention-seeking behavior was typical for the boy. Whether it was because his parents paid more attention to his younger brother and two younger sisters or there was another reason, the boy craved attention and no amount ever seemed to be good enough.[1]

If this was a typical child who wouldn't later be diagnosed with anti-social personality disorder, a Board-Certified Behavior Analyst (BCBA) would likely suggest to the boy's family and friends that they give him a significant amount of positive attention for the positive things he did. For example, patting him on the back when he answered a question correctly in class, thanking him when he did the dishes at home, or saying "yes" when he asked a peer to play or be friends. People who crave attention like this boy want any type of attention- positive or negative. This means the attention he received from the entire town when he was "missing" was likely thrilling, intoxicating, and incredibly reinforcing. The science of Applied Behavior Analysis would say that we need to give less attention to behaviors such as running away and more attention to behaviors such as any attempt to make friends or fit in.[1]

Maybe that would have worked. Or maybe it wouldn't have changed anything at all. What matters is that no amount of well-timed praise or attention can reliably override entrenched antisocial traits once they're established, and pretending otherwise places too much faith in intervention while ignoring real risk. By the time the boy's behavior escalated beyond childhood mischief, the question was no longer how to redirect him, but whether anyone was willing to take his danger seriously.[1]

The boy got older but his behaviors remained the same. Tests showed he was of low-normal intelligence and teachers said he was lazy, although he still managed decent scores in first and second grade. The school nurse noted that he continued to run away from home and that he frequently brought an iron bar on the bus to hit younger children with. A mental health evaluation that took place when he was about eight-years-old said that the boy seemed to feel as though no one could tell him what to do. He was angry at the attention his younger siblings and cousins gave, and he felt that his mother rejected and punished him for no reason. The report ended in a confidential note that said the nurse had spoken to the boy's parents about his behaviors and they were unconcerned and seemed to feel it was the school's problem to solve, not theirs. By the end of early childhood, his behaviors were no longer isolated or developmentally curious, but persistent, escalating, and already pointing toward a pattern that adults around him chose not to confront.[1]

CHAPTER 41

The boy turned nine in 1954 and everything that could go wrong, did go wrong.

Ten years after the newspaper article that outed their marriage, Thelma sent a letter to Arthur's parents claiming that she was Arther's legitimate wife and the two had a child together, one that was just one year older than the boy. The boy's grandparents showed this letter to his mother, Betty, and to say she was livid would be a great understatement. In a letter the boy wrote later, he said, "From that day forward my life turned upside down... Mom took over and she made life hell in that house."[1]

If they were happy before, they never were again. Arthur was ashamed and lived the rest of his life with his head down, hardly daring to look anyone in the eye. Meanwhile, Betty became a screamer and her husband couldn't even watch TV without being yelled at or having something thrown at his head. Extended family members said they watched her go from being a decent wife and mom to a negative, bitter woman whose new favorite word was "whore." On more than one occasion, Betty broke off a branch from one of the trees outside and whipped the boy with it. She also enjoyed using a long paddle and a toilet brush to hit him with. No matter what he did, he couldn't ever seem to earn his mother's love. Later, he said that his mother had only told him she loved him once in her life: "I love you only because you're my firstborn."[1]

If Betty turned cold and cruel after finding out about her husband's previous life, Arthur seemed to disappear. He couldn't do anything right at home, so he spent less and less time there. He busied himself at work and with making repairs around the house. He talked less, smoked more, and let his wife take over.[1]

Around this same time, the boy had his first sexual introduction. His aunt allegedly (she denies these claims)[2] often walked around in only her bra and underwear, enjoying the attention the nine-year-old gave her when she did so. She soon escalated to fondling him and then taught him some more explicit sexual acts, which was the beginning of the boy's obsession with sex that would continue throughout his entire life. After she left, he continued masturbating any chance he got. Around this time he also began engaging in inappropriate sexual behavior with his younger sister, Jeannie. However, he has gone back and forth on this claim, sometimes admitting to it and other times saying it was just a fantasy.[1]

One time while playing by himself, the boy fell and got stuck in a swamp. After crying for help, a boy named Mike showed up and helped him out of the swamp. They found a nearby creek where the boy took off his clothes, rinsed them off, then hung them on a bush to dry. Mike took his clothes off and joined him in the creek. Once they were out of the creek and drying off in the sun, the boy started masturbating and Mike followed his example. Whether it was the boy or Mike who initiated it, they then started touching each other and performing oral sex. This began a new and exciting friendship for the boy, who would meet Mike often and engage in this type of behavior with his new friend. The boys also engage in bestiality, or sex with animals, at a farm nearby. The boy later said, "it felt good at the time," and would continue this behavior in the years to come.[1]

By the time the boy was in eighth grade, he had flunked multiple grades and was three years older than his peers. It wasn't necessarily a lack of intelligence as much as it was a lack of caring or trying that caused his trouble in school. His classmates remember him as getting in trouble more than anyone else, repeating "die die die" as he walked, and randomly letting out loud, cackling laughs. The boy also started becoming more violent. He began setting fires, hitting kids and throwing things at them when they made him mad, and tormenting animals. Family members remember him skinning fish and seeing how long it would take for them to die, and there are also reports of abuse to cats, squirrels, chipmunks, frogs, and birds. In addition to this, he continued engaging in bestiality with chickens, cows, dogs, and a horse.[1]

The boy tried multiple different sports, from wrestling to baseball to football to lacrosse to track and field. In wrestling, he was too angry to be any good; he reacted violently whether he lost—throwing chairs at opponents— or won, continuing to attack them and injuring others with dangerous throws. In track, he shoved opponents out of their lanes, turning the event into something closer to a contact sport.[1]

As the boy's violence and recklessness grew, so did his propensity for injury. He suffered a hairline fracture after being hit in the skull by a discus thrown from fifteen feet away, spending several days in the hospital. In the following years, he was rendered unconscious by a shorted electrical switch, knocked out for half an hour by a sledgehammer, hospitalized overnight after falling from the top of a forty-foot ladder, and hospitalized again when struck by a truck, each incident adding to the cumulative trauma to his brain and foreshadowing the dangerous patterns to come.[1]

In addition to violence, the boy turned to thievery and peeping. He routinely stole things such as fruits and vegetables from the neighborhood farmers, money from the church offering, and food and money from grocery stores and gas stations. He also spied on his sisters, parents, and neighbors through windows or holes he drilled into the walls, excitedly telling his peers when he watched any of them having sex. When he was 14, he walked home from the bus stop and was stopped by a man in a convertible who offered to give him a ride home. Once he got inside, the teenager claimed that the man grabbed him by the throat and demanded that he pull his pants down. He then performed oral sex on the teenager and raped him afterward out of anger because the teenager seemed less than thrilled and this was unsatisfactory to the man. The teenager didn't tell anyone what had happened.[1]

CHAPTER 42

The teenager got older and supposedly wiser but still struggled to make friends. His behavior was strange and unpredictable. He would suddenly sprint, walk in perfectly straight lines, make exaggerated movements when standing, and dance wildly at parties, all long after being told it wasn't funny. He also continued his thieving ways, getting arrested in December 1963 at age 18 after attempting to rob the local Sears. After telling the judge he was caught up in the Christmas spirit and was simply trying to get some Christmas gifts for his family, he was sentenced to an 18-month probationary period.[1]

During his probation the teenager worked many different jobs, one of which was in a stockroom at a bargain center. It was here that he would meet what would become his first wife, Sarah. The two got married in September of 1964 and moved into a trailer on Sarah's parents' land. Although newly married, the two did not act like newlyweds. Friends and relatives noted that he seemed uninterested in his wife, spending more time flirting with waitresses at diners after work than with his wife at home. A few weeks after the wedding, he told a cousin that he still hadn't consummated the marriage.[1]

Clearly, that dry period didn't last long, as the couple had their son in October of the following year. One of the young man's cousins came by soon after to congratulate the two on the birth, and the young man tried to get his cousin to have sex with his wife, stopping just short of forcing it to happen. Later that same day, the young man and his cousin went for a drive when a kid threw a snowball at their car. The young man flew into a rage, chasing the kid home and breaking the door down so he could beat up the kid in his own house. The young man was arrested and thrown in jail for three days with an additional six months of probation (his original probationary period had just ended) and a mental health clinic found him to be emotionally unstable with disproportionate reactions to minor stress.[1]

After this incident, Sarah requested a divorce, tired of constantly moving due to the young man's inability to keep a job. The two officially split in August 1966, and by April 1967, he was seeing the woman who would become his second wife, Linda. That same month, he was drafted into the Army, where he quickly learned that he had to follow the rules or face the consequences. By September, he and Linda were married.[1]

It was in Vietnam that the young man got his first taste of the murder and brutality that would define his life a few years later. By his own account, the young man often went off on his own searching for "the enemy" with no one checking in on where he was. Every Vietnamese he found, he killed, regardless of age or gender. The more he found, the more brutal he became, graduating to binding, raping, and slicing into the women he found before letting them die. "All and all I know for a fact, I killed 39 people in Vietnam. Scared a lot and wounded more!" Upon his homecoming, he excitedly told stories to anyone who would listen of his days in Vietnam murdering and raping "the enemy" and how he only had to pay $2 to have sex with teenage sex workers.[1]

In the spring of 1969, the young man was honorably discharged from the Army; he immediately put in a disability claim and was given a $23permonth disability pension. That same year, he began committing a series of property crimes, including arson and burglary, targeting commercial buildings in the area. Seven months after his discharge, his second marriage had ended in divorce, and he found himself serving a fiveyear sentence in prison for these offenses.

As his first parole hearing approached, a psychiatrist assessed the young man. The evaluation described him as an immature adolescent with a schizoid personality who had broken down under the stress of unemployment, job difficulties, and rejection by his wife. While the burglary was considered minor, his three arsons suggested latent homicidal intent that should not be underestimated. The psychiatrist recommended close supervision, emotional support, and immediate referral to a mental health clinic upon parole, noting that he could be a fair parole risk if psychiatric treatment and monitoring were provided.

On October 18, 1971, the young man was paroled for twenty-two months after his parents promised they would provide a place for him in their home and would do whatever they needed to help him get back on the straight and narrow. Unfortunately, this proved to be an impossible promise to keep. In the Spring of 1972, the young man met Jack Blake, a 10-year-old boy with "blond hair, freckles, big ears, and a pug nose" who loved fishing and was a mama's boy through and through. The teenager took Jack and his little brother fishing one day without their mother knowing, and she was furious when she found out about it. The next time the teenager showed up at their door, Jack's mother told him in no uncertain terms that he was not allowed to take her son fishing again. The teenager said, "yes ma'am" and walked away. A few days later, Jack asked his mother if he could go to a friend's house, to which she responded with the affirmative and he went off. Sadly, Jack would never make it to his destination.[1] The teenager kidnapped, sexually assaulted, and suffocated Jack, leaving his remains in the woods to be found several months later.[2]

Fast forward a couple of months, the teenager was at it again. Karen Hill was a beautiful little eight-year-old girl who was born on Father's Day and whose favorite song was "Joy to the World" by Three Dog Night. One evening, while her mother was getting ready, Karen wandered down the creek bed that the teenager happened to be fishing near. According to later interviews with the teenager, Karen reminded him of his sister, Jeannie, which for some reason made him really angry. He grabbed Karen and "lost control," raping and strangling her[2] and then covering her body with stones before leaving the scene.[1]

The teenager was arrested in October of 1972 and confessed to the murder of both Jack and Karen. He was sentenced to 25 years in prison on a first-degree manslaughter charge.

Contrary to what one would think, this was only the beginning.

CHAPTER 43

After six applications for parole and having served only 15 of the 25 years he was sentenced, Arthur Shawcross was released due to being "considered a very good prisoner."[1] According to the Executive Director of the state's parole division, Edward Elwin, Shawcross would have been released in 1989 regardless because of his good behavior and also due to his service in Vietnam, so he defended the early release of the prisoner despite what he would go on to do.[2]

In March 1988, Arthur Shawcross killed his third victim: Dorothy "Dotsie" Blackburn. Dotsie was a 27-year-old prostitute, mother of three, and cocaine addict with a boyfriend she loved getting high with. She knew she was in a high-risk career but stayed as safe as possible by maintaining a clientele of regulars, always staying in the same area, and sticking to oral sex. Dotsie's body was found after nine days.[3]

Anna "Ann" Marie Steffen was also a 27-year-old prostitute who was last seen alive July 8th (sources differ on whether it was 1988 or 1989). Ann was a drug addict who had spent the majority of her childhood caring for her half-sister, Tina, who was a paraplegic and who died in 1980. After the death of her sister, Ann seemed to lose direction and turned to drugs to give her life meaning.[3]

Dorothy Keeler was a 59-year-old alcoholic who was known to be suspicious of others, distrusting, and very wary of men. She had few friends and, sadly, no one noticed her missing for several months. It is suggested that she was last seen alive in July 1989.[3]

Patricia "Patty" Ives was 25 years old and described by high school friends as gentle, loving, and kind, if a little naive. She was addicted to drugs and working as an exotic dancer-turned-prostitute who frequently attempted to get clean but always seemed to find herself back where she started. The last day Patty was seen was September 29, 1989.[3]

30-year-old June Stott didn't follow the pattern of victimization, as she was homeless rather than a prostitute or addicted to drugs. June was mentally ill and would occasionally disappear without telling anyone,[4] so her boyfriend didn't think to report her disappearance for several weeks after the fact. She was last seen on October 23, 1989.[3]

Shawcross began killing at a faster pace after this, murdering seven women over the next two months. He strangled his victims, and many of their bodies bore bite marks, suggesting a level of rage and domination that far exceeded the act of killing itself. It was also suggested that he had a level of sexual dysfunction, as one prostitute who lived to tell the tale shared that Shawcross was unable to achieve orgasm unless she "played dead."[5]

Marie Welch was a 22-year-old prostitute who was last seen November 5, 1989. Unfortunately, there is not much information known about her. Frances Brown was a sweet, blonde, glasses-wearing 22-year-old high school dropout who left behind her two grandparents and a young daughter when she was last seen just six days later on November 11, 1989. Her hobbies included music and poetry, and she was described as a "wanderer."

By late 1989, several more women disappeared whose lives are now known mostly by dates and ages rather than stories. Kimberly Logan, age 30, was last seen around November 1989. Elizabeth "Liz" Gibson, age 29, was last seen on November 25, 1989. Darlene Trippi, age 32, was last seen on December 15, 1989. June Cicero, age 34, was last seen on December 17, 1989. Felicia Stephens, just 20-years-old, was last seen on December 28, 1989. Beyond these basic facts, very little reliable information exists about who these women were, how they grew up, or what mattered to them. That absence reflects how easily society dismissed them while they were alive, reducing them to risk factors instead of recognizing them as human beings. They were daughters, friends, and people with inner lives we will never fully know, and they did not deserve the endings they were given.

The police organized search parties to find the three missing women who disappeared at the end of December, Darlene, June, and Felicia. On January 2nd, an air team found a body near a creek; as they got closer they noticed a man standing nearby, who sprinted away when he spotted the helicopter. The man was quickly apprehended and found to be Arthur Shawcross. After hours of interrogation during multiple interviews he finally confessed to the murders, but not before telling the interrogators what each of the women had done to deserve their vicious ending.[8]

On February 1, 1991, Arthur Shawcross was sentenced to 250 years behind bars for the ten lives he was convicted of killing.[9] He died in prison on November 10, 2008 of natural causes at age 63-years-old.[8]

CHAPTER 44

Arthur Shawcross's psychology has been picked apart for decades, often in an effort to find a single explanation that could make sense of what he became. Researchers, clinicians, and commentators have pointed to everything from genetic anomalies to personality disorders, hoping one diagnosis might offer clarity or closure. But the truth is less tidy. His case sits at the intersection of biology, environment, and repeated reinforcement of violent behavior, none of which operate in isolation. To understand how Shawcross thought, justified, and escalated, we have to look at several psychological frameworks not as excuses, but as lenses, each offering a partial view into a mind shaped long before his crimes became public.

One of the most interesting findings from looking into Shawcross's psychology was not actually in his mental capacities but rather in his blood. After looking into his blood tests and uranalysis reports, scientists discovered that everything was within normal ranges except something called "kryptopyrrole," which was measured at ten times the normal amount.[1]

The unusually high amount of kryptopyrrole in Shawcross's blood indicates Pyrrole Disorder, which is a genetic condition that causes dramatic shifts in mood and often exists comorbid with bipolar, anxiety, and/or schizophrenia.

The condition can cause things such as irritability, severe anxiety, short tempers, depression, inability to manage daily stress, and more. Interestingly enough, highly stressful events can also increase the risk of the negative effects that come alone with Pyrrole Disorder.[2]

Alongside elevated kryptopyrrole levels in his blood, Shawcross was also found to have an extra Y chromosome, a condition known as 47,XYY syndrome, or Jacob's syndrome. Jacob's syndrome is an incredibly rare congenital condition that creates an increased chance of a lot of the same traits as Pyrrole Disorder such as depression, anxiety, and learning disorders. Individuals with this condition also have an increased risk of behavioral issues such as aggression and impulsivity.[2] Research on criminals with XYY chromosomes has described individuals marked by extreme instability and irresponsibility, with behavior driven by immediate impulses rather than long-term consequences. Despite average intelligence, they tend to show shallow emotional connections, poor frustration tolerance, unrealistic planning, and a limited ability to understand and adapt to everyday social demands.[1]

The fact that Arthur Shawcross had these conditions does not automatically mean he was predestined to become a serial killer. Biological and biochemical theories can help explain vulnerability, but they do not account for the full picture. To understand how those vulnerabilities may have translated into behavior, it is necessary to look beyond chromosomes and chemistry and examine the psychiatric patterns that shaped how he related to others, regulated emotion, and responded to stress over time.

In the psychiatric evaluation of Arthur Shawcross, Dr. Dorothy Lewis, a forensic psychiatrist, proposed that he suffered from dissociative identity disorder (DID), arguing that extreme dissociation shaped his behavior and he should be institutionalized rather than imprisoned. Her theory was backed by stories Shawcross had told her about his childhood and adolescence, suggesting that his mother had sodomized him and he had cannibalized men and women in Vietnam. Her theories were further proven after putting Shawcross under hypnosis, when he took on several different personalities including his mother ("Bessie") and a reincarnated cannibal from 13th-century England named Ariemes.[3] While this theory may very well be true, it was heavily scrutinized as a convenient defense strategy rather than a credible clinical conclusion, with critics arguing that the diagnosis relied too heavily on Shawcross's own unverified accounts and behaviors that emerged only under hypnosis. Many experts viewed it less as a rigorous psychiatric finding and more as an attempt to medicalize brutality in a way that could soften legal responsibility, a framing the court ultimately rejected.[1]

If DID was controversial, the seemingly obvious diagnosis of antisocial personality disorder (ASPD) was only slightly less so. While everyone who heard of Shawcross unanimously agreed that he was an obvious ASPD case, those who met and spent time with him were less convinced. Psychiatrist Dr. Richard Kraus said, "when I met him I expected to find a pure sociopath– sinister, perverted, sly, evil, satanic. Instead… he looked [like] somebody's nice old uncle. I couldn't imagine a multiple murderer being so at ease in jail. It was as though he were welcoming you to his home. And almost the first words out of his mouth were that he was guilty as hell, a very unsociopathic thing to say."[1]

Despite that first impression, Kraus came to believe the friendliness was part of the problem, not evidence against it. He saw Shawcross as someone who could appear calm, likable, and cooperative while still lacking real empathy or remorse. Kraus also noted that Shawcross tended to tell people what he thought they wanted to hear, shifting his stories depending on his audience. This made diagnosis harder, but it did not change the larger pattern. In Shawcross's case, antisocial personality disorder did not look loud or threatening. It looked comfortable, familiar, and disturbingly easy.[4]

A diagnosis is only as helpful as the direction it gives us moving forward. In Arthur Shawcross's case, it certainly helped shine the light on excess kryptopyrrole and XYY chromosomes and it gave us an inside look at what other presentations of antisocial personality disorder can look like. However, at least 13 lives still had to end to learn this.

In the words of Dr. Richard Cross: "Arthur Shawcross was not 'born bad,' but the influences which shaped his life and behaviors were beyond his awareness and control. He was born with an unusual combination of predispositions to violence."[1] Understanding those predispositions does not excuse his actions, but it does force us to confront a harder truth: knowledge only matters if it is used early enough to prevent harm, not after the damage is already done.

PART 10

A TRUE POLITICIAN

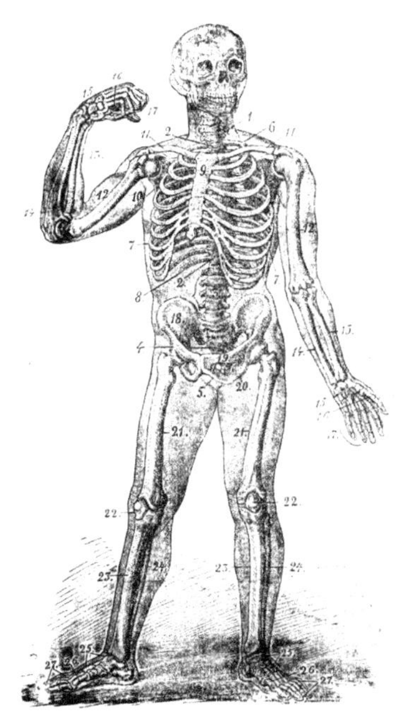

CHAPTER 45

It was a slightly chilly but average 42 degree day on March 17, 1942 when the boy was born to John and Marion. John was the fifth of seven children born in Chicago to Polish immigrants who migrated to the United States shortly before their eldest child was born.[2] He was an auto-repair machinist who took pride in what he viewed as traditional manhood, valuing physical toughness, self-reliance, emotional restraint, and rigid gender roles as markers of strength and respectability. As such, he took it upon himself to make sure his family knew these values by using his fists anytime they stepped out of line. He drank heavily and was the "punitive parent," frequently beating his son and calling him names such as "sissy."[1] Later, his son said this of his father: "He was Jekyll and Hyde when he drank. If he came up from the basement and said that the walls were pink, you said the walls were pink, but you learned to stay away from him and keep your mouth shut at the dinner table."[2]

John served in the U.S. Army's 132nd Infantry Regiment during World War I[2], a unit that fought in some of the war's bloodiest battles. Life in the 132nd meant months of trench warfare, constant shelling, and the daily reality of watching men around you be wounded or killed. Soldiers came home not just exhausted, but changed, often carrying invisible psychological wounds alongside physical ones. Many struggled with anger, emotional distance, and a need for rigid control long after the war ended.[3] John likely came home from this profoundly violent war and never truly left it behind.

The boy's mother, Marion, was born in Wisconsin and was the youngest of five children in a family that had strong Catholic values.[2] There's little else known about her except that she was frequently the victim of her husband's anger. One example of this happened just weeks after Marion had come home from the hospital with the couple's newest child, when John knocked three of his wife's teeth out. Marion ran outside but John followed her and continued beating her until the police arrived and intervened, eventually sending the battered wife back to her abusive husband.[4]

All of this meant the boy grew up in a household with a domineering father who had a very specific view of what being a man meant and a submissive mother who was gentle and loving but felt largely powerless to challenge her husband. If his father wasn't drunk when he got home from work, he would be soon. He usually went straight to the basement and began constructing things out of wood, refusing to let the boy join him except to put him to work. On the occasions when the boy did join him, he couldn't seem to do anything right. Whether he made an incorrect cut, let the paint drip onto the floor, or so much as dropped a screw on the ground, he was berated for his mistakes.[5] When the boy wasn't in the basement with his father, family members sometimes heard John talking to himself, often using voices that weren't his own. It's not known whether he had any mental diagnoses, but the behavior suggests a volatile, unpredictable presence that would shape the household and leave a lasting impression on his son.[2]

As much as John tried to keep his son from joining him in the basement, the boy wanted a relationship with his father so badly that nothing could keep him out. The more time the two spent together, though, the more the boy was told what a weak, inadequate, sissy boy he was, and the more the boy internalized these characteristics.[5] The humiliation that stemmed from these one-sided conversations likely stayed with the boy throughout his entire life and affected everything he would go on to do.

The boy grew and began becoming more aware of his sexuality, especially as early sexual experiences matured him far too quickly in this area. One of his first reported instances of abuse occurred when he was between the ages of six and ten, when a teenage family friend took him upstairs, undressed him, and molested him. On another occasion at around the same age, he was molested by a male contractor who was another friend of the family. Both of these occasions shaped who he would eventually become and would go on to be core experiences in his life.[7]

Despite telling him as a boy that he would "probably grow up queer,"[6] the boy's father had expected a traditionally masculine son and was extraordinarily disappointed with his son who was naturally drawn to other boys the older he got. However, the more violent his father got toward him, the more loving and nurturing his mother became. He grew closer to his mother and began stealing her underwear and wearing it, enjoying how silky and soft it was.[5] Some sources say that his mother found out and threatened to humiliate him if he ever did it again but refused to tell her husband out of fear for what he would do.[2] Others say that his mother made him put the underwear on to embarrass him and that he was whipped with a leather strap when his father found out.[4] Regardless, his homosexual tendencies and attraction toward women's intimates were not approved of by either of his parents.

As if the abusive father and parents who wouldn't accept his homosexual attractions weren't enough, by the end of grade school the boy was also regularly experiencing seizures and fainting spells and was diagnosed with a condition called recurrent syncope, which would eventually lead to temporal lobe epilepsy.[4] Syncope refers to a brief fainting episode caused by a temporary drop in blood flow to the brain. It comes on suddenly, lasts only a short time, and resolves on its own, but it often leads to emergency medical evaluations because it can look alarming and occur repeatedly.[8] Temporal lobe epilepsy, on the other hand, is the most common type of focal epilepsy that causes seizures. Over time, epilepsy can lead to lasting changes in how the brain functions, including irreversible neurocognitive decline, meaning learning, memory, focus, and decision making can become increasingly difficult. The risk of complications grows the longer seizures continue and the more frequently they occur, including depression, anxiety, significant memory loss, and in rare cases sudden unexplained death in epilepsy.[9]

Between the boy's complicated family relationships and his health issues, his childhood was marked by chaos, instability, and a persistent lack of control. Rather than safety or consistency, he experienced an environment where power was unpredictable and security was fragile, shaping a worldview rooted in confusion, fear, and a need to regain control.

CHAPTER 46

As a teenager, he continued dealing with his seizures and fainting spells. In one instance, he was at a friend's house when he had a seizure and his friend's parents, sure he was dying, quickly summoned a priest to give him his last rites.[1] He also continued struggling not with his sexuality but with his father's response to his sexuality. He began having relationships with boys, unbeknownst to his father, and having oral sex with them. However, this was complicated because even though the boys he was in relationships with were doing what he wanted them to do, meaning oral sex, he thought less of them because they were saying "yes" to him and complying. They were no longer "good" people in his mind.[2] In simple terms, the teenager took the negative feelings he had about himself and pushed them onto the boys instead. Even though they were doing exactly what he wanted, he judged them harshly for it, seeing their compliance as a flaw. This allowed him to feel more powerful and in control, while avoiding responsibility for his own actions and feelings.

The teenager got older and was able to get out from under his father's thumb. He started making his own decisions for the first time in his life without consciously fearing his father's opinion. In his early 20s he got his first job as a salesman, met his first wife, and had his first kid. As one would expect from an eventual serial killer who found his success manipulating people, the young man was an excellent salesman who could talk anyone into buying anything. Despite his father-in-law never quite taking a liking to him, he was seen by neighbors as a loving and caring husband and a devoted father to his son. His reputation could not have shone brighter in that little town of Springfield, Illinois.[1]

In 1966, the young man moved his small family to Waterloo, Iowa, where he exaggerated his resume just a smidge and was able to take over management of three separate Kentucky Fried Chicken stores that his father-in-law, Fred, needed help running. While Fred still didn't care for the young man, this job was an opportunity to be closer to his daughter, who had chosen her husband and loved him regardless of what her father said. It seems the young man's new employees didn't favor him anymore than Fred did, though, as they never seemed to be able to take him seriously and still saw Fred as their true boss. If it hadn't been for his daughter, Fred would have fired the "braggart and liar" immediately. Unfortunately, he had to accept the boy as a permanent fixture in his life if he wanted to keep his daughter close.[1]

With the young man feeling as though he was constantly being disrespected by his employees and his father-in-law, he turned to the Junior Chamber to fill his social needs, where he quickly found success. He became fast friends with Clarence Lane, the pseudonym for the man who would soon become the president of their local chapter, and this friendship cemented his love and affinity for politics. It didn't take Lane long to realize how gifted the young man was in talking people into things, and he decided to use that skill to his advantage and that of the Junior Chamber. Within one day of working with Lane, the young man had recruited 12 new members to their chapter. Soon, he was elected as chaplain and was holding regular prayer breakfasts. His extracurricular activities within the Junior Chamber, however, were somewhat less holy than his title would lead one to believe.[1]

Many individuals within the Junior Chamber were involved in the more permissive side of their town, which included prostitution, pornography, and other activities. The young man owned a motel that happened to be central to many of the illicit happenings, and so he, too, was heavily involved in casual sex and prostitution. While he was still married, he was often heard bragging about having sex with female employees or guests of his motel, although at least one of the women he had sex with had a less than favorable review of him. When he was with his wife in public, people later said there didn't seem to be any affection between the two, and he frequently offered her sexual services to other men, naming his "price" a blowjob.[1]

Another fascination of the young man's was first responders and the power associated with emergency situations. He liked to follow directly behind emergency vehicles with a flashing red light on the top of his car. It was important to him that he be known as someone who had influence with first responders, and he solidified this by giving them free fried chicken a few times a month. However, while he wanted to be known as being on the right side of the law, he also wanted people to see him as powerful and above the law, practicing this by taking young male employees out to steal car parts while he monitored the police radio.[1]

The young man was widely seen as incredibly charitable and successful in nearly everything he did. He had a knack for getting things done and could persuade almost anyone to support whatever business venture he was promoting at the time. He also gave generously, ensuring that children who would otherwise have nothing had money and food at Christmastime. On the flip side, plenty of people saw him in a far less favorable light, recognizing his boastful, manipulative, and calculating manner. One man saw him as a "kid trying to make it in an adult world" and his father-in-law saw him as a man who told people exactly what they wanted to hear but wasn't particularly charming if you saw through it. The chief of police thought the boy was a "wimp and a coward" who didn't like being told what to do and was a bad loser, and a local county attorney said he cared more about winning and being right than he cared about his own life or the lives of others.[1]

CHAPTER 47

Despite his rather polarizing personality, the man continued finding success everywhere he went, even when it came to getting in trouble with the law. In 1967, he cleverly devised a scheme to satisfy his sexual needs without being labeled a homosexual. He did this by setting up a "social club" in the basement of the restaurant where the boys who worked for him were able to pay a small monthly fee to play pool, drink beer, and participate in "experiments." The boys were told that the governor of Illinois had hired him to conduct experiments involving giving and receiving blowjobs. Naturally, he told them that in any other environment homosexual relationships were wrong (unless both participants were willing and didn't believe they were wrong) and this was strictly for science. If the boys didn't believe him, he pulled out his certificate attesting to the authenticity of the scheme.[1]

One night, the man invited a 16-year-old named Edward Lynch to his home to play pool, watch some movies, drink some beer, and participate in his experiment. This time, they made a deal while playing pool that the loser of the game would have to give the winner a blowjob. Lynch ended up winning the game but refused the blowjob and this angered the man greatly. He took the teenager upstairs while wielding a carving knife and attempted to wrestle him onto the bed where it is assumed he would rape him. Before the worst could happen, he accidentally cut Lynch on the arm and panicked, apologizing profusely and taking him back downstairs. In the basement, after persuading Lynch to stay, the man suggested another "experiment" where he chained him up, straddled him, and began rubbing his thighs. Lynch was able to push the man off of him, which again angered him and the man began choking him until he thought Lynch had blacked out. Lynch, who had been laying completely still and pretending he was unconscious, continued laying there until the agitated man asked if he was okay. Lynch then pretended to slowly wake up and asked to be taken home, to which the boy agreed.[1]

Lynch didn't immediately tell his parents or anyone in authority about the assault, but when talking with a friend about it, he discovered that he wasn't the only one who had been assaulted by the man. Donald Voorhees, Jr. was 15 years old when he was paid $50 to assist the man in sex education "research." Across several months, the man forced Voorhees to give him blowjobs, often after getting him drunk first. The man would then debrief with Voorhees, asking how the oral sex made him feel and showering him with money and gifts afterward.[1]

After discovering that neither boy was alone in their experiences, the two decided to tell their parents and then the police on March 11, 1968. On May 2nd, following several interviews, polygraph tests, and a meeting of the grand jury, the man was indicted on a charge of sodomy. The indictment sent shockwaves through the community, which found itself deeply divided. While some believed the accusations brought forward by Voorhees and Lynch, many others struggled to reconcile them with the image of the boy as a respected, generous, and upstanding member of the community, making it difficult for them to believe he could be capable of such acts.[1]

Shortly after the indictment, the man was driving around breaking and entering businesses with one of his younger employees, Russell Schroeder, when Schroeder began lamenting about his recent breakup. The man offhandedly suggested Schroeder do something to take the edge off. Like, perhaps, beating up a young teenager named Donald Voorhees, Jr. Schroeder agreed and the boy gave him a can of mace. One afternoon a few days later, Schroeder showed up at Voorhees' school, introduced himself as a "big brother," drove Voorhees out to an empty park, and sprayed him in the face with the can of mace. When Voorhees, disoriented but coherent, asked what was going on, Schroeder told him some guy named Jim paid him $10 to scare the 15-year-old because he suspected him of stealing tires. Immediately afterward, Voorhees went to the police and identified Schroeder as his attacker. While Schroeder initially denied the claim and kept the man's name out of it, he eventually came clean and told the police the whole plan from start to finish.[1]

In September, the man was sent to a psychiatric hospital for evaluation and made quite the impression on everyone there. In the 17 days he was there, he appeared friendly and cooperative on the surface while firmly denying all allegations and accepting no responsibility for his actions. Staff noted dramatic mood swings, shifting from crying to boasting to depression, as well as persistent manipulation of attendants to gain privileges and control over others. He blamed everyone but himself, rationalized every failure, expressed open hostility toward others, and showed no remorse for admitted behavior. The evaluating psychiatrist concluded that he habitually distorted the truth to protect his image, viewed himself as a constant victim, and was primarily motivated by outwitting and exploiting those around him, leading to a diagnosis of antisocial personality disorder and the assessment that treatment was unlikely to be effective.[1]

On December 3, 1968, the man was sentenced to ten years in prison for sodomy. While in prison, he was the model of good behavior. He got a job in the kitchen, received his high school diploma, served as chaplain of the prison chapter of Junior Chamber, taught prisoners how to read stock tables and invest, and won the "Sound Citizen Award." During that time his divorce was also finalized, he lost custody of his children, and his father died, which were all huge blows to his ego. He applied for early release under supervision many times and, while few people believed he had really changed, he was finally released for parole on June 18, 1970, almost eight years early.[1]

The naysayers who didn't believe the man would ever change his ways ended up being right. Almost as soon as he was released, he went back to his old ways of "engaging in homosexual activity." In one particular instance, Mickel Reid, age 20, met the man and went with him to his mother's apartment, where a sexual encounter occurred, and the two later went into business together doing painting and maintenance work. Soon after, Reid moved into the house the man lived in with his mother, during which time the boy spoke openly about violent fantasies involving handcuffing and beating young men, though Reid did not take them seriously. Over time Reid became increasingly uneasy, particularly after an incident in which he believed the boy intended to harm him. His fears were confirmed weeks later when the man struck him on the back of the head with a hammer in the garage, later stating he had felt a sudden urge to kill him. Reid moved out the following day.[1]

CHAPTER 48

On March 13,1980, after a five-week long trial, a jury of 12 took only two hours to convict John Wayne Gacy of 33 murders, sentencing him to death by lethal injection.[1] In the nine years between the Mickel Reid incident and the trial, Gacy continued to operate largely unchecked, embedding himself deeper into the community, refining his methods, and escalating the frequency and brutality of his crimes, all while maintaining the outward appearance of a successful, charitable, and trustworthy citizen.

Gacy's first known murder occurred in January 1972. After convincing 16-year-old Timothy McCoy to come to his house for sex, the two went to bed together for the last night of McCoy's life. The next morning Gacy saw McCoy standing in the doorway of his bedroom with a knife and, thinking he was going to attack him, rushed McCoy, attempting to wrestle the knife away and then stabbing him to death.[2] He dumped the teenager's body in the crawlspace under the trapdoor in his bedroom so no one would find him.[3] Later, he said the sexual gratification he received from that first murder was so intense and "that's when I realized that death was the ultimate thrill."[2]

Between that first murder and the moment he was caught, the primary method Gacy used involved cruising the streets of Chicago to find young men and boys, including sex workers, whom he would coax or force into going to his home. There, he would sexually assault and physically torture them, often using handcuffs and restraints, before strangling them to death. He typically concealed the bodies in the crawl space and basement of his house, burying many on the property and sometimes disposing of others elsewhere, allowing him to continue killing for years undetected.[4]

John Wayne Gacy was arrested in 1979 and his trial began in 1980, where he confessed to murdering at least 30 people. While he pleaded not guilty by reason of insanity, he was found guilty of 33 murders and was executed on May 10, 1994.[2]

While Gacy's methods and psychology have been extensively analyzed, far less attention has been given to the individuals whose lives he erased. These victims are often reduced to numbers, timelines, or footnotes, despite being the central human cost of his crimes, and it is unbelievable how hard it is to find even the names of these individuals. What information does exist about these victims is fragmented, uneven, and often painfully brief. Even so, these details matter. They reflect real people with lives, relationships, and futures that existed long before Gacy entered them.

Robert Piest was 15 years old when he went missing. About to walk out to the car where his mom sat waiting for him to take him home for her 46th birthday celebration, Piest asked for a few more minutes so he could talk to someone about a new, higher-paying job. That someone ended up being John Wayne Gacy, and Piest was never seen again.[6]

Francis Wayne Alexander would have been 21 or 22 when he was killed around 1976 or 1977, though he was not identified as a victim until 2021 through DNA. Born in North Carolina, he later lived in New York and then Chicago. Alexander had been married and divorced, worked in bars and clubs, and was loved by his family, including his sister Carolyn. At the time of his disappearance, he had limited contact with them, and no missing person report was filed because his absence was not immediately questioned.[5]

Robert Winch, 16, was born in Cleveland Ohio in 1961. His girlfriend had just dropped him off at McDonalds so he could meet up with a friend, when Gacy approached him about a job. Winch had four brothers and one sister who still lived at home when he disappeared in 1977.[7]

James Haakenson was a runaway from Minnesota. He had recently been estranged from his family after coming out as gay.[6] In August 1976, he called his mother from Chicago, and she never heard from him again. Haakenson's disappearance left his family without answers for decades.[8]

Seventeen-year-old Rick Johnston was supposed to be attending a concert and had just been dropped off at the ballroom by his mom when he disappeared. He left behind his parents, Kenneth and Esther, and his two brothers, Mitch and Greg.[9]

Eighteen-year-old John Butkovich was an employee of Gacy who went to Gacy's home to collect a missing paycheck. A Croatian American, Butkovich was known as hardworking and quick to learn, and he was reportedly close to Gacy's family. Those who knew him remembered his dedication and quiet determination.[10]

Over the six years between 1972 and 1978, John Wayne Gacy took the lives of at least 33 young men and boys, ranging in age from 14 to 23, leaving behind families, friends, and futures that would never be realized. Among them were Timothy Jack McCoy, 16; John Butkovich, 18; Darrell Julius Samson, 18; Randall Wayne Reffett, 15; Samuel Dodd Stapleton, 14; Michael Lawrence Bonnin, 17; William Huey Carroll Jr., 16; James Byron Haakenson, 16;

Rick Louis Johnston, 17; Kenneth Ray Parker, 16; Michael M. Marino, 14; William George Bundy, 19; Francis Wayne Alexander, 21; Gregory John Godzik, 17; John Alan Szyc, 19; Jon Steven Prestidge, 20; Matthew Walter Bowman, 19; Robert Edward Gilroy Jr., 18; John Antheney Mowery, 19; Russell Lloyd Nelson, 21; Robert David Winch, 16; Tommy Joe Boling, 20; David Paul Talsma, 19; William Wayne Kindred, 19; Timothy David O'Rourke, 20; Frank William Landingin, 19; James Mazzara, 20; and Robert Jerome Piest, 15. Five additional victims remain unidentified, known only by their approximate ages and the years they were killed. Each of these young men, whether named or not, represents a life interrupted, a family left grieving, and the human cost of violence that should never be forgotten.[11]

CHAPTER 49

The terrifying part of John Wayne Gacy is how truly awful his crimes were combined with how involved he was in his community. After getting engaged for the first time, Gacy began managing three KFC restaurants that his future father-in-law owned, and he managed these restaurants throughout his entire criminal career. After involving himself in the Junior Chamber, he got into politics and became the Democratic precinct captain in a Chicago suburb. His reasoning for getting into politics was that he "was always looking for acceptance, and my dad made me feel that I was never good enough." He was well-respected in his community and was able to gain a lot of influence through the gatherings he assembled and organizations he was involved in.[1] Through these roles, he gained respect and influence, leveraging community events and organizations to establish a polished public image.

Gacy also belonged to a Chicago-area group called the Jolly Jokers and often entertained at children's parties, charity events, and other gatherings in full clown costume and makeup, using the personas "Pogo the Clown" and "Patches the Clown." While under police surveillance years later, he told detectives that his work as a clown allowed him to get away with murder, highlighting how he exploited his public persona to conceal his crimes.[1]

The two lives this "Killer Clown" lived calls attention to the tension between his outward, socially acceptable life and his secret, violent behavior. After 65 hours of psychiatric interviews, Dr. Richard G. Rappaport concluded that Gacy was criminally insane and had a "borderline personality organization with the subtype of psychopathic personality and with episodes of and an underlying paranoid schizophrenia." The personality traits that backed up this conclusion were Gacy's angry and impulsive eruptions, depression characterized by loneliness, a lack of identity, chaotic sexual relations, and gross denial of any wrongdoing. He also said that Gacy had an "unusual degree of self-reference" and desperately needed to be loved and admired, using his charming nature to manipulate others in his roles of politician and clown.[2]

Other experts, however, disagreed with the notion of insanity. Gacy was also examined by doctors at a prestigious medical center who concluded that not only was he not insane at the time of the murders, but he also had no mental illness that would have prevented him from understanding the severity of what he had done. They diagnosed him with mixed personality disorder, which included obsessive-compulsive disorder, antisocial personality, and narcissistic personality disorder.[2]

Gacy's upbringing offers further context for his behavior. From the beginning he was set up for failure by a father who was domineering and never demonstrated anything even close to love for his son. He was emotionally abused and made to believe he was worthless by the one person who was supposed to unconditionally love him, so his sole goal in life was to prove that he did matter. Gacy's sexual assaults were motivated more by the need to assert dominance and prove he was worthy than by sexual desire. Murder became the ultimate way to demonstrate power and control over victims who were completely defenseless and to debunk his father's opinion of him.[2]

This pattern is supported by formal measures of psychopathy. The Hare Psychopathy Checklist-Revised (PCL-R) is a forensic tool that evaluates psychopathy using 20 traits, each scored 0 to 2, for a maximum of 40 points. A score over 30 generally indicates psychopathy. Gacy scored a 36 out of 40 on the PCL-R, an extraordinarily high score that identifies him as an extreme psychopath, indicating a complete lack of empathy, remorse, or true emotional connection. Gacy consistently used charm and confidence as tools rather than genuine social connection. He presented himself as important, trustworthy, and likable, while lying easily and often manipulating others for personal gain. He showed little to no remorse for the harm he caused and demonstrated a profound lack of empathy, viewing other people as objects to control rather than individuals with inherent worth. Emotionally, his responses were shallow and self-focused, and he showed poor behavioral control alongside a long pattern of rule-breaking and criminal behavior. While he was capable of maintaining jobs and relationships on the surface, these were unstable beneath the façade and served his needs rather than reflecting meaningful attachment. Taken together, these traits describe someone who could convincingly function in society while simultaneously engaging in repeated, extreme violence without guilt, accountability, or concern for others.[3]

John Wayne Gacy's story is a chilling reminder of how extreme violence can hide behind charm, community involvement, and public trust. Beneath the surface of the well-known, influential, and respected man was a criminal so horrendous he is widely known as one of the deadliest and most notorious serial killers of all time. However, the flip side of this notoriety is how painfully little we know about his victims. John Wayne Gacy will forever have a place in our history books, while the 33+ lives he took will slowly be erased from our memory. Understanding Gacy's psychology highlights his calculated cruelty, but it is the human lives he destroyed that make his pathology truly devastating.

CHAPTER 50

BLUEPRINT OF A KILLER

There's an age-old question about how serial killers are created: Are they born, or are they made? Genetics certainly play a role, but the environment a child grows up in is arguably the most crucial factor in shaping who they will become as an adult. Early experiences of love, touch, and safety- or the lack of them- literally shape a child's brain, emotional regulation, and ability to connect with others, which can have lifelong consequences.

When you think back to your earliest childhood memories, I'm willing to bet you still have your first landline number memorized, you can still remember how to get to your childhood best friend's house, and you can still use the sign language you learned for fun during indoor recess in second grade (was that just me?). You also probably have clear memories of the first time you got spanked, your first heartbreak, and the first time you got caught lying or cheating on a test. If those times we're able to remember have such a huge effect on us, imagine how much the times we can't remember affect us.

According to studies, the most important developmental period of an individual's life is early infancy.[1] All those things that happened to you before you could remember? Those are arguably the most important moments of your life when it comes to development. What happens during pregnancy and the first few years of life does not just shape childhood, it shapes adulthood. Experiences in those early years literally get built into the body and brain, for better or worse. The first six years are especially critical. When things go well, kids are more likely to grow into healthier adults who can learn, regulate emotions, and function socially. When there are disruptions like abuse, neglect, or instability, it can affect behavior, learning, and even physical health decades later.

The environment that the child grows up in and the individuals that are most present in the child's life are what play the most vital role. One study[3] found that out of 200 convicted killers, 25% had a history of physical abuse in their childhoods, 43% had parents that rejected them or treated them with cruelty. Another study[4] looked at 105 serial killers and found that 35% had some history of death in their family, 13 of the serial killers had family members who committed suicide. These numbers aren't exactly comforting because there are still many killers who didn't have these risk factors. This reminds us that while childhood experiences matter a great deal, they are not destiny. Many children who face adversity go on to lead healthy, successful lives, and most children who grow up in difficult circumstances do not become violent offenders. Understanding risk factors is about giving support where it's needed, not assuming a dark future is inevitable.

The good news is this is not a lost cause. Acting early and acting often matters. Early supports like quality childcare, parent education, family support, and reducing financial stress do more than help in the moment. They change life trajectories and pay off far more than they cost. One of the easiest ways to support childhood development from the very moment of birth is in positive touch such as hugging, holding, appropriate kissing, etc. Research has shown that positive touch when a child is in infancy affects self-regulation and supports development of social competence. In contrast, when a child grew up in a home where they received negative touch, a lack of affection, and/or corporal punishment, they are more likely to grow into adults who have more trouble getting along with others and who withdraw or are socially opposed. Overall, positive touch has shown to predict healthier, more social, and more well-rounded adults.[5]

So, what does all of this mean? Serial killers are not born fully formed; they are the result of a complex mix of biology, environment, and chance. Childhood matters. The love, attention, and safety, or the lack thereof that a child experiences literally shapes the wiring of their brain and the patterns of their heart. But it's important to remember that even in the darkest stories, there are exceptions. Many children who endure adversity grow up to be healthy, caring adults. Childhood is powerful, yes, but it is not destiny.

The real takeaway is prevention, intervention, and support matter. By understanding the factors that increase risk, society has the opportunity to provide children with the tools, safety, and nurture they need to grow into well-adjusted adults. Positive touch, emotional attunement, stable relationships, and early support can literally change the course of a life. If there is hope in this research, it is here: even small acts of care can have lifelong impact. How we treat our children today can echo across a lifetime, and maybe, just maybe, prevent the next tragedy before it starts.

"The more healthy relationships a child has, the more likely he will be to recover from trauma and thrive. Relationships are the agents of change and the most powerful therapy is human love."[6]

BIBLIOGRAPHY

Intro:

1. Marono, A. J., S. Reid, E. Yaksic, and D. A. Keatley. "A Behaviour Sequence Analysis of Serial Killers' Lives: From Childhood Abuse to Methods of Murder." *Psychiatry, Psychology, and Law: An Interdisciplinary Journal of the Australian and New Zealand Association of Psychiatry, Psychology and Law* 27, no. 1 (2020): 126–137. https://doi.org/10.1080/13218719.2019.1695517.

2. Narvaez, D., L. Wang, A. Cheng, T. R. Gleason, R. Woodbury, A. Kurth, and J. B. Lefever. "The Importance of Early Life Touch for Psychosocial and Moral Development." *Psicologia, Reflexão e Crítica: Revista Semestral do Departamento de Psicologia da UFRGS* 32, no. 1 (2019): 16. https://doi.org/10.1186/s41155-019-0129-0.

3. Perry, Bruce D., and Maia Szalavitz. *The Boy Who Was Raised as a Dog: And Other Stories from a Child Psychiatrist's Notebook What Traumatized Children Can Teach Us About Life, Loss, Love, and Healing.* New York: Basic Books, 2008.

Chapter 1:

1. Giannetakis, Paola. "Behavioral Patterns and Genesis of a Polymorphous Paraphilic Serial Killer." *Journal of Forensic Science & Criminal Investigation* 6, no. 1 (2017): 555683. https://doi.org/10.19080/JFSCI.2017.06.555683.

2. DiMaggio, C., L. S. Sun, A. Kakavouli, M. W. Byrne, and G. Li. "A Retrospective Cohort Study of the Association of Anesthesia and Hernia Repair Surgery with Behavioral

and Developmental Disorders in Young Children." *Journal of Neurosurgical Anesthesiology* 21, no. 4 (2009): 286–291. https://doi.org/10.1097/ANA.0b013e3181a71f11.

3. Jia, X., S. Tan, Y. Qin, Y. Wei, Y. Jiang, S. Pan, C. Li, J. Chen, T. Liu, and Y. Xie. "Experiencing Anesthesia and Surgery Early in Life Impairs Cognitive and Behavioral Development." *Frontiers in Neuroscience* 18 (2024): 1406172. https://doi.org/10.3389/fnins.2024.1406172.

4. The Lantern. "Jeffrey Dahmer: A Look into the Past." *The Ohio State University Archives,* August 1, 1991. https://osupublicationarchives.osu.edu/?a=d&d=LTN19910801-01.2.12.

5. Dahmer, L. *A Father's Story.* William Morrow & Company, 2025.

Chapter 2:

1. Dahmer, L. *A Father's Story.* William Morrow & Company, 2025.

2. Kong, R., R. Chen, and L. Meng. "Parental Conflict and Adolescents' Socially Adverse Emotions: The Mediating Role of Family Functioning." *Frontiers in Psychology* 15 (2024): 1387698. https://doi.org/10.3389/fpsyg.2024.1387698.

3. Federal Bureau of Investigation. "Jeffrey Lionel Dahmer, Part 03." *FBI Vault.* https://vault.fbi.gov/jeffrey-lionel-dahmer/Jeffrey%20Lionel%20Dahmer%20Part%2003/view.

Chapter 3:

1. PBS. "Milestones in the American Gay Rights Movement." *American Experience.* Accessed October 9, 2025. https://www.pbs.org/wgbh/americanexperience/features/stonewall-milestones-american-gay-rights-movement/.

2. The Inner Life of a Psycho Killer. *Chicago Reader.* Accessed October 9, 2025. https://chicagoreader.com/news/the-inner-life-of-a-psycho-killer/.

3. Longobardi, C., and L. Badenes-Ribera. "Intimate Partner Violence in Same-Sex Relationships and the Role of Sexual Minority Stressors: A Systematic Review of the Past 10 Years." *Journal of Child and Family Studies* 26, no. 8

(2017): 2039–2049. https://doi.org/10.1007/s10826-017-0734-4.

4. Federal Bureau of Investigation. "Jeffrey Lionel Dahmer, Part 01." *FBI Vault.* https://vault.fbi.gov/jeffrey-lionel-dahmer/Jeffrey%20Lionel%20Dahmer%20Part%2001/view.

5. Dahmer, L. *A Father's Story.* William Morrow & Company, 2025.

Chapter 4:

1. Bertram, C. "Jeffrey Dahmer: A Timeline of His Murders, Arrests and Death." *Biography*, April 3, 2025. https://www.biography.com/crime/a64379331/jeffrey-dahmer-timeline.

2. Journal Sentinel. "Jeffrey Dahmer's 17 Victims and What We Knew About Them: Errol Lindsey, Rita Isbell, Anthony (Tony) Hughes." *Journal Sentinel*, September 28, 2022. https://www.jsonline.com/story/news/2022/09/28/jeffrey-dahmers-17-victims-and-what-we-knew-them-errol-lindsey-rita-isbell-anthony-tony-hughes/10443235002/.

Chapter 5:

1. American Psychiatric Association. *Diagnostic and Statistical Manual of Mental Disorders.* 5th ed. Arlington, VA: American Psychiatric Publishing, 2013.

2. Cleveland Clinic. "Amygdala: What It Is and What It Controls." Cleveland Clinic. April 11, 2023. Accessed October 10, 2025. https://my.clevelandclinic.org/health/body/24894-amygdala.

3. Federal Bureau of Investigation. "Jeffrey Lionel Dahmer, Part 03." FBI Vault. Accessed October 10, 2025. https://vault.fbi.gov/jeffrey-lionel-dahmer/Jeffrey%20Lionel%20Dahmer%20Part%2003/view.

4. Hare, R. *The Psychopathy Checklist-Revised.* 2nd ed. Toronto: Multi-Health Systems, 2003.

5. Konrad, M. *Dark Minds, Deadly Deeds: Unmasking Serial Killers.* Accessed October 10, 2025. https://csi.pressbooks.pub/darkmindsdeadlydeeds/.

6. Ramsland, K. "Are All Serial Killers Psychopaths?" *Psychology Today*, April 9, 2025. https://www.psychology-

today.com/us/blog/shadow-boxing/202504/are-all-serial-killers-psychopaths.

7. The Inner Life of a Psycho Killer. *Chicago Reader*. Accessed October 9, 2025. https://chicagoreader.com/news/the-inner-life-of-a-psycho-killer/.

8. Yang, Y., A. Raine, K. L. Narr, P. Colletti, and A. W. Toga. "Localization of Deformations Within the Amygdala in Individuals With Psychopathy." *Archives of General Psychiatry* 66, no. 9 (2009): 986–994. https://doi.org/10.1001/archgenpsychiatry.2009.110.

Chapter 6:

1. Slade, T., ed. *The Unfinished Autobiography of Aileen Wuornos*. 2021.

2. National Scientific Council on the Developing Child. *The Science of Neglect: The Persistent Absence of Responsive Care Disrupts the Developing Brain: Working Paper 12.* 2012. http://www.developingchild.harvard.edu.

3. Raine, A., P. Brennan, and S. Mednick. "Birth Complications Combined With Early Maternal Rejection at Age 1 Year Predispose to Violent Crime at Age 18 Years." *Archives of General Psychiatry* 51, no. 12 (1994): 984–88.

4. Smith, A. "The 'Monster' in All of Us: When Victims Become Perpetrators." *Suffolk University Law Review* 38, no. 2 (2005): 367–394. https://scholarship.law.georgetown.edu/cgi/viewcontent.cgi?article=1218&context=facpub.

5. Investigation Discovery. *Mind of a Monster: Aileen Wuornos*, episodes 1–5 [YouTube playlist]. YouTube. https://www.youtube.com/watch?v=EMaN49NEj9o&list=PL5ZSqdgaeKOwmzvq6MZmSgxuYr_RUq6r-.

Chapter 7:

1. Slade, T., ed. *The Unfinished Autobiography of Aileen Wuornos*. 2021.

2. Smith, A. "The 'Monster' in All of Us: When Victims Become Perpetrators." *Suffolk University Law Review* 38, no. 2 (2005): 367–394. https://scholarship.law.georgetown.edu/cgi/viewcontent.cgi?article=1218&context=facpub.

3. Russell, S. *Damsel of Death: The Inside Story of the World's First Female Serial Killer*. True Crime, 1992.

4. Investigation Discovery. *Mind of a Monster: Aileen Wuornos*, episodes 1–5 [YouTube playlist]. YouTube. https://www.youtube.com/watch?v=EMaN49NE-j9o&list=PL5ZSqdgaeKOwmzvq6MZmSgxuYr_RUq6r-.

Chapter 8:

1. Smith, A. "The 'Monster' in All of Us: When Victims Become Perpetrators." *Suffolk University Law Review* 38, no. 2 (2005): 367–394. https://scholarship.law.georgetown.edu/cgi/viewcontent.cgi?article=1218&context=facpub.

2. *Wuornos v. State*, 644 So. 2d 1000 (Fla. 1994). https://law.justia.com/cases/florida/supreme-court/1994/79484-0.html.

3. Tampa Bay Times. "Victims of Aileen Wuornos." October 9, 2002. https://www.tampabay.com/archive/2002/10/09/victims-of-aileen-wuornos/.

4. Meloy, J., and A. Fetthous. "Serial Murder and the Case of Aileen Wuornos: Attachment Theory, Psychopathy, and Predatory Aggression." *Behavioral Sciences & the Law* 22, no. 3 (2004): 375–393.

Chapter 9:

1. Investigation Discovery. *Mind of a Monster: Aileen Wuornos*, episodes 1–5 [YouTube playlist]. YouTube. https://www.youtube.com/watch?v=EMaN49NE-j9o&list=PL5ZSqdgaeKOwmzvq6MZmSgxuYr_RUq6r-.

2. Freedman, R., S. Leonard, A. Olincy, C. Kaufmann, D. Malaspina, C. Cloninger, D. Svrakic, S. Faraone, and M. Tsuang. "Evidence for the Multigenic Inheritance of Schizophrenia." *American Journal of Medical Genetics Part A* 105, no. 8 (2001): 794–800.

3. Myers, W., E. Gooch, and J. Meloy. "The Role of Psychopathy and Sexuality in a Female Serial Killer." *Journal of Forensic Sciences* 50, no. 3 (2005): 652–657.

4. Ma, G., H. Fan, C. Shen, and W. Wang. "Genetic and Neuroimaging Features of Personality Disorders: State of the Art." *Neuroscience Bulletin* 32, no. 3 (2016): 286–306.

5. Smith, A. "The 'Monster' in All of Us: When Victims Become Perpetrators." *Suffolk University Law Review* 38, no. 2 (2005): 367–394. https://scholarship.law.georgetown. edu/cgi/viewcontent.cgi?article=1218&context=facpub.

6. Wilson, H., and C. Widom. "The Role of Youth Problem Behaviors in the Path From Child Abuse and Neglect to Prostitution: A Prospective Examination." *Journal of Research on Adolescence* 20, no. 1 (2010).

7. Meloy, J., and A. Fetthous. "Serial Murder and the Case of Aileen Wuornos: Attachment Theory, Psychopathy, and Predatory Aggression." *Behavioral Sciences & the Law* 22, no. 3 (2004): 375–393.

Chapter 10:

1. Prăvălie, R. "Nuclear Weapons Tests and Environmental Consequences: A Global Perspective." *Ambio* 43, no. 6 (2014): 729–744. https://doi.org/10.1007/s13280-014-0491-1.

2. Kamani, H., M. Baniasadi, H. Abdipour, L. Mohammadi, S. Rayegannakhost, H. Moein, and A. Azari. "Health Risk Assessment of BTEX Compounds (Benzene, Toluene, Ethylbenzene and Xylene) in Different Indoor Air Using Monte Carlo Simulation in Zahedan City, Iran." *Heliyon* 9, no. 9 (2023): e20294. https://doi.org/10.1016/j.heliyon.2023.e20294.

3. Carlo, P. *The Night Stalker: The Life and Crimes of Richard Ramirez.* Citadel Press, 2016.

4. Marsh, Laura, and Gregory L. Krauss. "Aggression and Violence in Patients with Epilepsy." *Epilepsy & Behavior* 1, no. 3 (2000): 160–168. https://doi.org/10.1006/ebeh.2000.0061.

Chapter 11:

1. Carlo, P. *The Night Stalker: The Life and Crimes of Richard Ramirez.* Citadel Press, 2016.

2. Doyle White, E. "Satanism: Definition, Beliefs, Symbols, & Anton LaVey." In *Encyclopaedia Britannica*, November 4, 2025. https://www.britannica.com/topic/Satanism.

3. Šram, Z. "Psychopathy and Depression as Predictors of the Satanic Syndrome." *Open Theology* 3, no. 1 (2017): 90–106. https://doi.org/10.1515/opth-2017-0007.

Chapter 12:

1. Carlo, P. *The Night Stalker: The Life and Crimes of Richard Ramirez.* Citadel Press, 2016.

2. Borch, F. L. "What Really Happened on 16 March 1968? What Lessons Have Been Learned? A Look at the My Lai Incident Fifty Years Later." Army Historical Foundation, 2018. https://armyhistory.org/my-lai/.

3. The New York Times. "Cocaine and Hollywood: Suspicions Are Rife." July 11, 1978. https://www.nytimes.com/1978/07/11/archives/cocaine-and-hollywood-suspicions-are-rife.html.

4. CBS News. "Richard Ramirez: The Story, the Evidence, the Night Stalker [Photo-Essay]." Accessed December 19, 2025. https://www.cbsnews.com/pictures/richard-ramirez-night-stalker-murders/.

Chapter 13:

1. Carlo, P. *The Night Stalker: The Life and Crimes of Richard Ramirez.* Citadel Press, 2016.

2. Lallanilla, M. "Case File: Richard Ramirez." A&E Television Networks, September 5, 2025. https://www.aetv.com/articles/richard-ramirez.

3. Restore Mental Health. "The Nightstalker's Mental Health: A Look into Richard Ramirez's Psychological Profile." Accessed December 19, 2025. https://restore-mental-health.com/night-stalker-mental-health/.

4. UPI. "Transcript of Ramirez Remarks at Sentencing." November 7, 1989. https://www.upi.com/Archives/1989/11/07/Transcript-of-Ramirez-remarks-at-sentencing/7642626418000/.

Chapter 14:

1. Carlo, P. *The Night Stalker: The Life and Crimes of Richard Ramirez.* Citadel Press, 2016.

2. Restore Mental Health. "The Nightstalker's Mental Health: A Look into Richard Ramirez's Psychological Profile." Accessed December 19, 2025. https://restore-mental-health.com/night-stalker-mental-health/.

3. Cleveland Clinic. "What's the Difference between Psychopathy and Sociopathy?" Cleveland Clinic, May 14, 2025. https://health.clevelandclinic.org/psychopath-vs-sociopath.

4. Cleveland Clinic. "Narcissistic Personality Disorder: Symptoms & Treatment." Cleveland Clinic, August 3, 2023. https://my.clevelandclinic.org/health/diseases/9742-narcissistic-personality-disorder.

5. Brown, G. R. "Sexual Sadism Disorder." In *Merck Manual Professional Edition.* October 2025. https://www.merck-manuals.com/professional/psychiatric-disorders/paraphilias-and-paraphilic-disorders/sexual-sadism-disorder.

Chapter 15:

1. Schechter, H. *Hell's Princess: The Mystery of Belle Gunness, Butcher of Men.* Little A, 2018.

2. Ammeson, J. S. *America's Femme Fatale: The Story of Serial Killer Belle Gunness.* Red Lightning Books, 2021.

3. Myhre, J. E. "Emigration from Norway, 1830–1920." Nordics.info, September 8, 2021. https://nordics.info/show/artikel/emigration-from-norway-1830-1920.

4. Bengtsson, E. "Inequality and the Working Class in Scandinavia 1800 to 1910: Workers' Share of Growing Incomes." *Investigaciones de Historia Económica – Economic History Research* 14, no. 3 (2018): 170–180. https://doi.org/10.1016/j.ihe.2017.11.004.

5. Sampson, R. J., and J. H. Laub. "Urban Poverty and the Family Context of Delinquency: A New Look at Structure and Process in a Classic Study." *Child Development* 65, no. 2 (1994): 523–540.

6. Kim, H. H., K. A. McLaughlin, L. B. Chibnik, K. C. Koenen, and H. Tiemeier. "Poverty, Cortical Structure, and Psychopathologic Characteristics in Adolescence." *JAMA Network Open* 5, no. 11 (2022): e2244049. https://doi.org/10.1001/jamanetworkopen.2022.44049.

7. Lund, C., A. Breen, A. J. Flisher, R. Kakuma, J. Corrigall, J. A. Joska, L. Swartz, and V. Patel. "Poverty and Common Mental Disorders in Low and Middle Income Countries: A Systematic Review." *Social Science & Medicine* 71, no. 3 (2010): 517–528. https://doi.org/10.1016/j.socscimed.2010.04.027.

Chapter 16:

1. Ammeson, J. S. *America's Femme Fatale: The Story of Serial Killer Belle Gunness.* Red Lightning Books, 2021.

2. Schechter, H. *Hell's Princess: The Mystery of Belle Gunness, Butcher of Men.* Little A, 2018.

Chapter 17:

1. Ammeson, J. S. *America's Femme Fatale: The Story of Serial Killer Belle Gunness.* Red Lightning Books, 2021.

2. Schechter, H. *Hell's Princess: The Mystery of Belle Gunness, Butcher of Men.* Little A, 2018.

3. "Indiana's Murder Farm." *Harper's Weekly*, Vol. LII, No. 268 (May 30, 1908): 23.

Chapter 18:

1. Ammeson, J. S. *America's Femme Fatale: The Story of Serial Killer Belle Gunness.* Red Lightning Books, 2021.

2. Hinton, P. K. "Just Like One of the Family: An Immigrant Murderess in Turn-of-the-Century America." *Ohio Valley History* 6, no. 4 (2006): 27–47. https://muse.jhu.edu/article/573099.

3. Horspool, David. "Belle Gunness: The Early 20th Century Female Serial Killer You Probably Haven't Heard Of." A&E Television Networks, July 7, 2017. https://www.aetv.com/articles/belle-gunness-the-early-20th-century-female-serial-killer-you-probably-havent-heard-of.

4. Schechter, Harold. *Hell's Princess: The Mystery of Belle Gunness, Butcher of Men.* New York: Little A, 2018.

5. *The Washington Herald.* "Untitled Article." May 10, 1908. Library of Congress. https://www.loc.gov/item/sn83045433/1908-05-10/ed-1/.

Chapter 19:

1. Flashner, G. "Why There Are Fewer Female Serial Killers Than Male Killers in the U.S." *A&E*, November 7, 2025. https://www.aetv.com/articles/why-there-are-fewer-female-serial-killers-than-males-in-the-united-states.

2. Harrison, Marissa A., Erin A. Murphy, Laura Y. Ho, Thomas G. Bowers, and Christine V. Flaherty. "Female Serial Killers in the United States: Means, Motives, and Makings." *Journal of Forensic Psychiatry & Psychology* 26, no. 3 (2015): 383–406. https://doi.org/10.1080/14789949.2015.1007516.

Chapter 20:

1. Anne Rule. *Green River, Running Red: The Real Story of the Green River Killer—America's Deadliest Serial Murderer*. New York: Pocket Books, 2004.

2. Roman A. Koposov, Andrew Stickley, Jonas Isaksson, and Vladimir Ruchkin. "Enuresis in Young Offenders: A Study on Prevalence and Mental Health Comorbidity." *Frontiers in Psychiatry* 15 (2024). https://doi.org/10.3389/fpsyt.2024.1328767.

3. Karestan C. Koenen, Terrie E. Moffitt, Andrea L. Roberts, Lori T. Martin, Laura Kubzansky, HonaLee Harrington, Richie Poulton, and Avshalom Caspi. "Childhood IQ and Adult Mental Disorders: A Test of the Cognitive Reserve Hypothesis." *American Journal of Psychiatry* 166, no. 1 (2009): 50–57. https://doi.org/10.1176/appi.ajp.2008.08030343.

4. Norm Maleng. *Prosecutor's Summary of the Evidence: State of Washington vs. Gary Leon Ridgway (Case No. 01-1-10270-9)*. Seattle: Superior Court of Washington for King County, 2003. https://murderpedia.org/male.R/images/ridgway_gary/reports/summary.pdf.

Chapter 21:

1. Harden, Blaine. "The Banality of Gary: A Green River Chiller." *Washington Post*, November 15, 2003. https://www.washingtonpost.com/archive/lifestyle/2003/11/16/the-banality-of-gary-a-green-river-chiller/2d9575c7-6843-4ec3-9517-72cd3ecdd9b0/.

2. Keppel, Robert D., William J. Birnes, and Ann Rule. *The Riverman: Ted Bundy and I Hunt for the Green River Killer*. Rev. and updated ed. New York: Pocket Books, 2005.

3. Maleng, Norm. *Prosecutor's Summary of the Evidence: State of Washington vs. Gary Leon Ridgway (Case No. 01-1-10270-9)*. Seattle: Superior Court of Washington for King County, 2003. https://murderpedia.org/male.R/images/ridgway_gary/reports/summary.pdf.

4. Meloy, J. Reid. "The Nature and Dynamics of Sexual Homicide: An Integrative Review." *Aggression and Violent Behavior* 5, no. 1 (2000): 1–22. https://drreidmeloy.com/wp-content/uploads/2015/12/2000_TheNatureAndDyn.pdf.

5. Rule, Ann. *Green River, Running Red: The Real Story of the Green River Killer—America's Deadliest Serial Murderer*. New York: Pocket Books, 2004.

Chapter 22:

1. Keppel, Robert D., William J. Birnes, and Ann Rule. *The Riverman: Ted Bundy and I Hunt for the Green River Killer*. Rev. and updated ed. New York: Pocket Books, 2005.

2. Harden, Blaine. "The Banality of Gary: A Green River Chiller." *Washington Post*, November 15, 2003. https://www.washingtonpost.com/archive/lifestyle/2003/11/16/the-banality-of-gary-a-green-river-chiller/2d9575c7-6843-4ec3-9517-72cd3ecdd9b0/

Chapter 23:

1. Harden, Blaine. "The Banality of Gary: A Green River Chiller." *Washington Post*, November 15, 2003. https://www.washingtonpost.com/archive/lifestyle/2003/11/16/the-banality-of-gary-a-green-river-chiller/2d9575c7-6843-4ec3-9517-72cd3ecdd9b0/.

2. Maleng, Norm. *Prosecutor's Summary of the Evidence: State of Washington vs. Gary Leon Ridgway (Case No. 01-1-10270-9)*. Seattle: Superior Court of Washington for King County, 2003. https://murderpedia.org/male.R/images/ridgway_gary/reports/summary.pdf.

3. Castillo, Natalie V. *A Case Study on the First Five Victims of the Green River Killer*. Master's thesis, Seattle Univer-

sity, 2020. https://scholarworks.seattleu.edu/cgi/viewcontent.cgi?article=1001&context=wgst-theses

4. Rule, Ann. *Green River, Running Red: The Real Story of the Green River Killer, America's Deadliest Serial Murderer*. New York: Pocket Books, 2004.

5. Smith, Carlton, and Tomas Guillen. 2001. "Green River Suspect Fits FBI's Profile." *The Seattle Times*, December 16, 2001. https://archive.seattletimes.com/archive/20011216/profiles16m/green-river-suspect-fits-fbis-profile/

6. King County Sheriff's Office. *Green River Homicides Investigation*. King County, Washington. Accessed December 19, 2025. https://kingcounty.gov/en/dept/sheriff/courts-jails-legal-system/sheriff-services/investigations/green-river

7. Green, Sara Jean. "Green River Killer: Timeline and Victims." *The News Tribune* (Tacoma, WA), June 8, 2014. Accessed December 27, 2025. https://www.thenewstribune.com/news/special-reports/article25855165.html

Chapter 24:

1. Harden, Blaine. "The Banality of Gary: A Green River Chiller." *Washington Post*, November 15, 2003. https://www.washingtonpost.com/archive/lifestyle/2003/11/16/the-banality-of-gary-a-green-river-chiller/2d9575c7-6843-4ec3-9517-72cd3ecdd9b0/.

2. Leary, Terence, Larry Southard, Hill,Joe, I.,II, and John Ashman. , 2017. "The Macdonald Triad Revisited: An Empirical Assessment of Relationships between Triadic Elements and Parental Abuse in Serial Killers," *North American Journal of Psychology* 19 (3): 627-640. https://www.proquest.com/scholarly-journals/macdonald-triad-revisited-empirical-assessment/docview/1967812947/se-2.

3. Rule, Ann. *Green River, Running Red: The Real Story of the Green River Killer, America's Deadliest Serial Murderer*. New York: Pocket Books, 2004.

4. Karestan C. Koenen, Terrie E. Moffitt, Andrea L. Roberts, Lori T. Martin, Laura Kubzansky, HonaLee Harrington, Richie Poulton, and Avshalom Caspi. "Childhood IQ and Adult Mental Disorders: A Test of the Cognitive

Reserve Hypothesis." *American Journal of Psychiatry* 166, no. 1 (2009): 50–57. https://doi.org/10.1176/appi.ajp.2008.08030343.

5.   Maleng, Norm. *Prosecutor's Summary of the Evidence: State of Washington vs. Gary Leon Ridgway* (Case No. 01-1-10270-9). Seattle: Superior Court of Washington for King County, 2003. https://murderpedia.org/male.R/images/ridgway_gary/reports/summary.pdf.

6.   CNN, "Green River Killer Sentenced to Life in Prison," *CNN*, December 18, 2003, https://www.cnn.com/2003/LAW/12/18/green.river.sentencing/.

Chapter 25:

*   *Note: The early life chapters draw primarily from Katherine Ramsland's extensive interviews and correspondence with Dennis Rader, which remain the most comprehensive primary source on his childhood and psychological development.*

1.   Ramsland, Katherine M. *Confession of a Serial Killer: The Untold Story of Dennis Rader, the BTK Killer.* Hanover, NH: University Press of New England, 2016

2.   Bonn, Scott A. "Evolution of a Serial Killer: Dennis Rader, BTK." *Psychology Today*, February 7, 2022. https://www.psychologytoday.com/us/blog/wicked-deeds/202202/evolution-serial-killer-dennis-rader-btk

3.   Roadside America. "World's Largest Ball of Twine, Cawker City, Kansas." *Roadside America.* Accessed December 21, 2025.   https://www.roadsideamerica.com/story/8543

Chapter 26:

1.   Capote, Truman. *In Cold Blood.* New York: Random House, 1966.

2.   Ramsland, Katherine M. *Confession of a Serial Killer: The Untold Story of Dennis Rader, the BTK Killer.* Hanover, NH: University Press of New England, 2016

3.   Haining, Peter. *The Classic Era of American Pulp Magazines.* Chicago: Chicago Review Press, 2001.

Chapter 27:

1. Ramsland, Katherine M. *Confession of a Serial Killer: The Untold Story of Dennis Rader, the BTK Killer.* Hanover, NH: University Press of New England, 2016

2. *State of Kansas v. Dennis L. Rader*, Case No. 05 CR 498, Guilty Plea Transcript, Sedgwick County District Court, June 27, 2005. Accessed December 23, 2025. https://murderpedia.org/male.R/images/rader_dennis/rader-testimony.pdf

3. Uncovered. "Dennis Rader, the BTK Killer: Timeline and Murders." *Uncovered.* Accessed December 23, 2025. https://uncovered.com/dennis-rader-btk/.

4. CNN. "Inside the Mind of BTK: Dennis Rader Details His Crimes." CNN, aired June 27, 2005. Transcript, CNN.com. Accessed December 23, 2025. https://transcripts.cnn.com/show/asb/date/2005-06-27/segment/01.

Chapter 28:

1. *State of Kansas v. Dennis L. Rader*, Case No. 05 CR 498, Guilty Plea Transcript, Sedgwick County District Court, June 27, 2005. Accessed December 23, 2025. https://murderpedia.org/male.R/images/rader_dennis/rader-testimony.pdf

2. Ramsland, Katherine M. *Confession of a Serial Killer: The Untold Story of Dennis Rader, the BTK Killer.* Hanover, NH: University Press of New England, 2016

3. Piccotti, Tyler. "A Timeline of the BTK Killer's Murders and How He Was Caught." *Biography.com.* Accessed December 23, 2025. https://www.biography.com/crime/a63496187/btk-killer-criminal-timeline

4. Finger, Stan. "'Bored,' Rader Decided to Resurface." *The Wichita Eagle*, originally published circa 2005; reposted on *Kansas.com.* Accessed December 23, 2025. https://www.kansas.com/news/special-reports/btk/article1003767.html

Chapter 29:

1. Hutnyan, Matthew S. "BTK: A Case Study in Psychopathy," *SMU Journal of Undergraduate Research* 7, no. 2 (2022): Article 5.

2. Mayo Clinic. "Antisocial Personality Disorder." Accessed December 23, 2025. https://www.mayoclinic.org/

diseases-conditions/antisocial-personality-disorder/symp-toms-causes/syc-20353928.

3. Mayo Clinic. "Obsessive-Compulsive Disorder." Accessed December 23, 2025. https://www.mayoclinic.org/diseases-conditions/obsessive-compulsive-disorder/symp-toms-causes/syc-20354432.

4. Mayo Clinic. "Narcissistic Personality Disorder." Accessed December 23, 2025. https://www.mayoclinic.org/diseases-conditions/narcissistic-personality-disorder/symptoms-causes/syc-20366662.

5. Ramsland, Katherine M. *Confession of a Serial Killer: The Untold Story of Dennis Rader, the BTK Killer.* Hanover, NH: University Press of New England, 2016

6. Katherine Ramsland, "Dr. Katherine Ramsland Explains How the BTK Killer's Mind Works," interview by Dr. Oz, Facebook video, February 2023, personal viewing

7. CNN. "BTK Suspect in Custody; Police Say They Have Serial Killer," *CNN*, February 28, 2005. Accessed December 23, 2025. https://www.cnn.com/2005/US/02/28/cnna.btk/index.html.

Chapter 30:

1. Englade, Ken. *Cellar of Horror: The Story of Gary Heidnik.* New York: St. Martin's Press, 1992.

2. Apsche, Jack A., and Jerry L. Jennings. *Breaking the Silence of the Lambs.* City: ePrinted Books, 2014.

3. UPI, "Father Offers to Hang Torture-Suspect Son," *United Press International*, March 27, 1987, accessed via UPI Archives, https://www.upi.com/Archives/1987/03/27/Father-offers-to-hang-torture-suspect-son/5404543819600/. upi.com

4. Mayo Clinic Staff, "Bed-wetting: Symptoms and Causes," *Mayo Clinic*, August 24, 2023, https://www.mayoclinic.org/diseases-conditions/bed-wetting/symptoms-causes/syc-20366685/. mayoclinic.org

5. Fiorillo, Victor. "Inside the House of Heidnik." *Philadelphia Magazine*, July 23, 2007. https://www.phillymag.com/news/2007/07/23/inside-the-house-of-heidnik/.

Chapter 31:

1. Apsche, Jack A., and Jerry L. Jennings. *Breaking the Silence of the Lambs*. City: ePrinted Books, 2014.

2. Englade, Ken. *Cellar of Horror: The Story of Gary Heidnik*. New York: St. Martin's Press, 1992.

3. van Sambeck, Becca. "Before Gary Heidnik Was Exposed as a 'Monster Preacher,' He Committed Another Shocking Crime." *Oxygen*, May 18, 2023. https://www.oxygen.com/monster-preacher/crime-news/monster-preacher-gary-heidniks-childhood-past-crimes/.

Chapter 32:

1. Apsche, Jack A., and Jerry L. Jennings. *Breaking the Silence of the Lambs*. City: ePrinted Books, 2014.

2. Englade, Ken. *Cellar of Horror: The Story of Gary Heidnik*. New York: St. Martin's Press, 1992.

3. van Sambeck, Becca. "Before Gary Heidnik Was Exposed as a 'Monster Preacher,' He Committed Another Shocking Crime." *Oxygen*, May 18, 2023. https://www.oxygen.com/monster-preacher/crime-news/monster-preacher-gary-heidniks-childhood-past-crimes/.

4. Janos, Adam. "Gary Heidnik's Unspeakable Crimes: An Interview with the Serial Killer's Attorney." *A&E Real Crime*, January 14, 2021. Accessed via Internet Archive, January 15, 2021. https://web.archive.org/web/20210115170047/https://www.aetv.com/real-crime/gary-heidnik

Chapter 33:

1. Apsche, Jack A., and Jerry L. Jennings. *Breaking the Silence of the Lambs*. City: ePrinted Books, 2014.

2. Englade, Ken. *Cellar of Horror: The Story of Gary Heidnik*. New York: St. Martin's Press, 1992.

3. van Sambeck, Becca. "After Surviving 'House of Horrors,' Where Are 'Monster Preacher' Gary Heidnik's Victims Today?" *Oxygen True Crime*, January 16, 2021. Accessed December 27, 2025. https://www.oxygen.com/monster-preacher/crime-news/monster-preacher-where-are-gary-heidniks-victims-today

Chapter 34:

1. *In re Gary Heidnik, Maxine Davidson White, Appellant, v. Martin Horn, Commissioner, Pennsylvania Department of Corrections, et al.*, 112 F.3d 105 (3d Cir. 1997), accessed via Justia, https://law.justia.com/cases/federal/appellate-courts/F3/112/105/585379/.

2. Apsche, Jack A., and Jerry L. Jennings. *Breaking the Silence of the Lambs*. City: ePrinted Books, 2014.

3. World Health Organization. *Schizophrenia*. Last updated October 6, 2025. Accessed December 26, 2025. https://www.who.int/news-room/fact-sheets/detail/schizophrenia.

Chapter 35:

1. Woodrow, Jane Carter. *Rose West: The Making of a Monster*. London: Hodder & Stoughton, 2012. ISBN 9780340992487.

Chapter 36:

1. Woodrow, Jane Carter. *Rose West: The Making of a Monster*. London: Hodder & Stoughton, 2012. ISBN 9780340992487.

Chapter 37:

1. Woodrow, Jane Carter. *Rose West: The Making of a Monster*. London: Hodder & Stoughton, 2012. ISBN 9780340992487.

Chapter 38:

1. Woodrow, Jane Carter. *Rose West: The Making of a Monster*. London: Hodder & Stoughton, 2012. ISBN 9780340992487.

2. Waxman, Olivia B. "The Chilling True Story Behind *Fred & Rose West: A British Horror Story*." *TIME*, May 14, 2025. https://time.com/7285264/fred-and-rose-west-true-story-netflix

3. BBC News. "The 12 Victims of Fred and Rosemary West." BBC News, May 27, 2021. https://www.bbc.com/news/ukenglandgloucestershire57182844

Chapter 39:

1. "Mental Education: Abnormal Psychology of Rosemary West," *Mental Education* (blog), September 22, 2021, https://mentaleducation.health.blog/2021/09/22/abnormal-psychology-of-rosemary-west/

2. Psychology Today. "Sadism." *Psychology Today*. Accessed [insert date you accessed it]. https://www.psychologytoday.com/us/basics/sadism

3. Downing, Nancy R., Marvellous Akinlotan, and Carly W. Thornhill. "The Impact of Childhood Sexual Abuse and Adverse Childhood Experiences on Adult Health Related Quality of Life." *Child Abuse & Neglect* 120 (2021): 105181. https://doi.org/10.1016/j.chiabu.2021.105181

4. Drury, Alan J., Michael J. Elbert, and Matt DeLisi. "Childhood Sexual Abuse Is Significantly Associated with Subsequent Sexual Offending: New Evidence among Federal Correctional Clients." *Child Abuse & Neglect* 95 (2019): 104035. https://doi.org/10.1016/j.chiabu.2019.104035

5. Zhang, Yun, TianTian He, and HaiFeng Shi. "Electroconvulsive Therapy in Pregnancy: A Systematic Review." *Archives of Women's Mental Health* 18, no. 1 (2015): 1–7. https://doi.org/10.1007/s0073701404771

6. Drury, Alan J., Michael J. Elbert, and Matt DeLisi. "Childhood Sexual Abuse Is Significantly Associated with Subsequent Sexual Offending: New Evidence among Federal Correctional Clients." *Child Abuse & Neglect* 95 (2019): 104035. https://doi.org/10.1016/j.chiabu.2019.104035

Chapter 40:

1. Olsen, Jack. *The Misbegotten Son: A Serial Killer and His Victims*. New York: Delacorte Press, 1993.

Chapter 41:

1. Olsen, Jack. *The Misbegotten Son: A Serial Killer and His Victims*. New York: Delacorte Press, 1993.

2. Morgan, Amber. "The Horrific Story of Arthur Shawcross, the 'Genesee River Killer' Who Murdered at Least 14 Victims." *AllThat'sInteresting.com*, October 27, 2024. Accessed January 4, 2026. https://allthatsinteresting.com/arthurshawcross

Chapter 42:

1. Olsen, Jack. *The Misbegotten Son: A Serial Killer and His Victims*. New York: Delacorte Press, 1993.

2. Morgan, Amber. "The Horrific Story of Arthur Shawcross, the 'Genesee River Killer' Who Murdered at Least 14 Victims." *AllThat'sInteresting.com*, October 27, 2024. Accessed January 4, 2026. https://allthatsinteresting.com/arthurshawcross

Chapter 43:

1. Hanley, Robert. "Parole Board Under Scrutiny in Murder Suspect's Release." *New York Times*, January 13, 1990

2. Tron, Gina. "'He Should Suffer': Why Was Serial Killer Arthur Shawcross Paroled Before Murder Spree?" *Oxygen.com*, November 20, 2020. Accessed January 4, 2026. https://www.oxygen.com/true-crime-buzz/crazy-not-insane-why-was-arthur-shawcross-released-early

3. Olsen, Jack. *The Misbegotten Son: A Serial Killer and His Victims*. New York: Delacorte Press, 1993.

4. Smith, Daniel. "Profile of Serial Killer Arthur Shawcross." *ThoughtCo*, August 13, 2020. Accessed January 5, 2026. https://www.thoughtco.com/profile-of-serial-killer-arthur-shawcross-973145

5. "Chapter Nine: The Making of a Serial Killer." In *Unknown Title*, SAGE Publications, 2019. Accessed January 5, 2026. https://au.sagepub.com/sites/default/files/upm-assets/91090_book_item_91090.pdf

Chapter 44:

1. Olsen, Jack. *The Misbegotten Son: A Serial Killer and His Victims*. New York: Delacorte Press, 1993.

2. Cherney, Kristeen. "Pyrrole Disorder: Symptoms, Causes, Diagnosis & Treatment." *Healthline*, updated February 21, 2023. https://www.healthline.com/health/pyrrole-disorder#causes

3. Foderaro, Lisa W. "A Serial-Murder Trial, On TV, Grips Rochester." *New York Times*, December 2, 1990.

4. Ramsland, Katherine. "Evaluations — Arthur Shawcross, the Genesee River Strangler." *Crime Library*, accessed

January 6, 2026. https://mail.crimelibrary.org/serial_killers/predators/shawcross/10.html

Chapter 45:

1. Adam Janos, "John Wayne Gacy's Childhood: 'Killer Clown' Serial Killer Was Victim of Abuse," *A&E Crime + Investigation*, September 15, 2020, last updated October 14, 2025, https://www.aetv.com/articles/john-wayne-gacys-childhood

2. Myers, Brian. "Who Were John Wayne Gacy's Parents?" *Medium*, October 2, 2023. https://medium.com/@brianjmyers/who-were-john-wayne-gacys-parents-6880630b275f

3. Davis, Abel. *The Story of the 132d Infantry, A.E.F.* Chicago: Pritzker Military Museum & Library, 1919.

4. Sullivan, Terry, and Peter T. Maiken. *Killer Clown: The John Wayne Gacy Murders*. Foreword by Gregg Olsen. New York: Citadel Press, Kensington Publishing Corp., 2023. ISBN 9780806542409

5. Rappaport, Dr. Richard. "John Wayne Gacy with Dr. Richard Rappaport." *Making a Monster: The Tapes*. Interview by *Crime and Investigation*. March 16, 2020. Podcast audio, 00:00:00. Apple Podcasts. https://podcasts.apple.com/de/podcast/john-wayne-gacy-with-dr-richard-rappaport/id1496132151?i=1000468515923

6. BuchananDunne, Michael J. "Infamous Murderer & Serial Killer Profiles #2 John Wayne Gacy." *Murder Mile Tours (blog)*, May 22, 2017. https://www.murdermiletours.com/blog/infamous-murderer-serial-killer-profiles-2-john-wayne-gacy#:~:text=Aged%20six%2C%20when%20Gacy's%20mother,other%20people's%20feelings%20and%20needs

7. Biography.com Editors. "John Wayne Gacy." *Biography.com*, October 16, 2025. https://www.biography.com/crime/john-wayne-gacy

8. Greve, Yvonne, Felicitas Geier, Steffen Popp, Thomas Bertsch, Katrin Singler, Florian Meier, Alexander Smolarsky, Harald Mang, Christian Müller, and Michael Christ. *"Syncope Prevalence in the Emergency Department Compared to General Practice and Population: A Strong Se-*

lection Process." Heart 101, no. 19 (2015): 1591-1599. https://doi.org/10.1136/heartjnl-2014-306599

9. Cleveland Clinic. 2025. *"Temporal Lobe Epilepsy (TLE): Causes, Symptoms & Treatment."* Cleveland Clinic. Last reviewed January 8, 2025. https://my.clevelandclinic.org/health/diseases/17778-temporal-lobe-seizures

Chapter 46:

1. Sullivan, Terry, and Peter T. Maiken. *Killer Clown: The John Wayne Gacy Murders*. Foreword by Gregg Olsen. New York: Citadel Press, Kensington Publishing Corp., 2023. ISBN 9780806542409

2. Rappaport, Dr. Richard. "John Wayne Gacy with Dr. Richard Rappaport." *Making a Monster: The Tapes*. Interview by *Crime and Investigation*. March 16, 2020. Podcast audio, 00:00:00. Apple Podcasts. https://podcasts.apple.com/de/podcast/john-wayne-gacy-with-dr-richard-rappaport/id1496132151?i=1000468515923

Chapter 47:

1. Sullivan, Terry, and Peter T. Maiken. *Killer Clown: The John Wayne Gacy Murders*. Foreword by Gregg Olsen. New York: Citadel Press, Kensington Publishing Corp., 2023. ISBN 9780806542409

Chapter 48:

1. Chicago Tribune. *"John Wayne Gacy: A Timeline of the Killer Clown's Life and Crimes."* Chicago Tribune, October 25, 2021. https://graphics.chicagotribune.com/john-wayne-gacy-new-timeline/blurb.html

2. Biography.com Editors, Colin McEvoy, and Catherine Caruso. *"John Wayne Gacy: Biography, Serial Killer, Killer Clown."* Biography.com, updated October 16, 2025. https://www.biography.com/crime/john-wayne-gacy#childhood

3. Wilkinson, Alec. 1994. *"Conversations with a Killer."* The New Yorker, April 18, 1994. https://www.newyorker.com/magazine/1994/04/18/conversations-with-a-killer

4. Luongo, Anthony J., III. *"John Wayne Gacy."* EBSCO Research Starters, 2022. https://www.ebsco.com/research-starters/history/john-wayne-gacy

5. WBEZ Chicago. 2021. "Another Victim of Serial Killer John Wayne Gacy Has Been Identified Using DNA." *WBEZ Chicago*, October 26, 2021. https://www.wbez.org/2021/10/26/another-victim-of-serial-killer-john-wayne-gacy-has-been-identified-using-dna

6. Manna, Nichole. 2025. "John Wayne Gacy's Capture Happened Because of a Missing Teen Case." *A&E*. October 15, 2025. https://www.aetv.com/articles/john-wayne-gacy-capture-missing-teen-case

7. Find A Grave. n.d. "Robert David Winch (1961–1977) Memorial." *Find A Grave*. Accessed January 14, 2026. https://www.findagrave.com/memorial/65099040/robert_david-winch

8. Cook County Sheriff's Office. 2017. "Unknown Gacy Victim Identified." *Cook County Sheriff's Office*, July 19, 2017. https://cookcountysheriffil.gov/unknown-gacy-victim-identified/

9. Find A Grave. n.d. "Rick Louis Johnston (1961–1978) Memorial." *Find A Grave*. Accessed January 14, 2026. https://www.findagrave.com/memorial/204678944/rick_louis-johnston

10. Wikipedia. n.d. "Murder of John Butkovich." *Wikipedia, The Free Encyclopedia*. Accessed January 14, 2026. https://en.wikipedia.org/wiki/Murder_of_John_Butkovich

11. *A Thousand Miles of True Crime*. 2022. "20. John Wayne Gacy: The Victims." Podcast audio, 1:04:00. August 2, 2022. Apple Podcasts. https://podcasts.apple.com/us/podcast/20johnwaynegacythevictims/id1596130481?i=1000574760573

Chapter 49:

1. Biography.com Editors, "John Wayne Gacy: Biography, Serial Killer, Killer Clown," *Biography.com*, October 16, 2025, https://www.biography.com/crime/johnwaynegacy

2. Sullivan, Terry, and Peter T. Maiken. *Killer Clown: The John Wayne Gacy Murders*. Foreword by Gregg Olsen.

New York: Citadel Press, Kensington Publishing Corp., 2023. ISBN 9780806542409

3. Michael Konrad, "John Wayne Gacy: Psychopathology & AntiSocial Personality Disorder," in *Dark Minds, Deadly Deeds: Unmasking Serial Killers*, ed. Michael Konrad, chapter 15, CSI Pressbooks, 2025, https://csi.pressbooks.pub/darkmindsdeadlydeeds/chapter/john-wayne-gacy-psychopathology-anti-social-personality-disorder/

Chapter 50:

1. Likhar, Akanksha, Prerna Baghel, and Manoj Patil. 2022. "Early Childhood Development and Social Determinants." *Cureus* 14, no. 9 (September 23). https://doi.org/10.7759/cureus.29500

2. Langevin, R., D. Paitich, B. Orchard, L. Handy, and A. Russon. 1983. "Childhood and Family Background of Killers Seen for Psychiatric Assessment: A Controlled Study." *Bulletin of the American Academy of Psychiatry and the Law* 11 (4): 331–343. https://jaapl.org/content/11/4/331.full.pdf

3. Wille, W. S. *Citizens Who Commit Murder*. St. Louis, MO: Warren H. Green, Inc., 1974.

4. Hill, D., and D. A. Pond. "Reflection on One Hundred Capital Cases Submitted to Electroencephalography." *Journal of Mental Science* 98 (1952): 23–43.

5. Narvaez, Darcia, Paul A. Hastings, Katrina L. Valentino, and Tracy P. I. Beilock. 2019. "The Importance of Early Life Touch for Psychosocial and Moral Development." *Psicologia: Reflexão e Crítica* 32 (Article 129). https://pmc.ncbi.nlm.nih.gov/articles/PMC6967013

6. Bruce D. Perry and Maia Szalavitz, *The Boy Who Was Raised as a Dog: And Other Stories from a Child Psychiatrist's Notebook* (New York: Basic Books, 2006), [30].

*For More News About Heather Mroczenski,
Signup For Our Newsletter:*

http://wbp.bz/newsletter

*Word-of-mouth is critical to an author's long-
term success. If you appreciated this book please
leave a review on the Amazon sales page:*

https://wbp.bz/blueprintofakillerr

ALSO PUBLISHED BY WILDBLUE PRESS

MOTHERS AND MURDERERS
BY KATHERINE ELLISON

https://wbp.bz/mothersmurderersa

ALSO PUBLISHED BY WILDBLUE PRESS

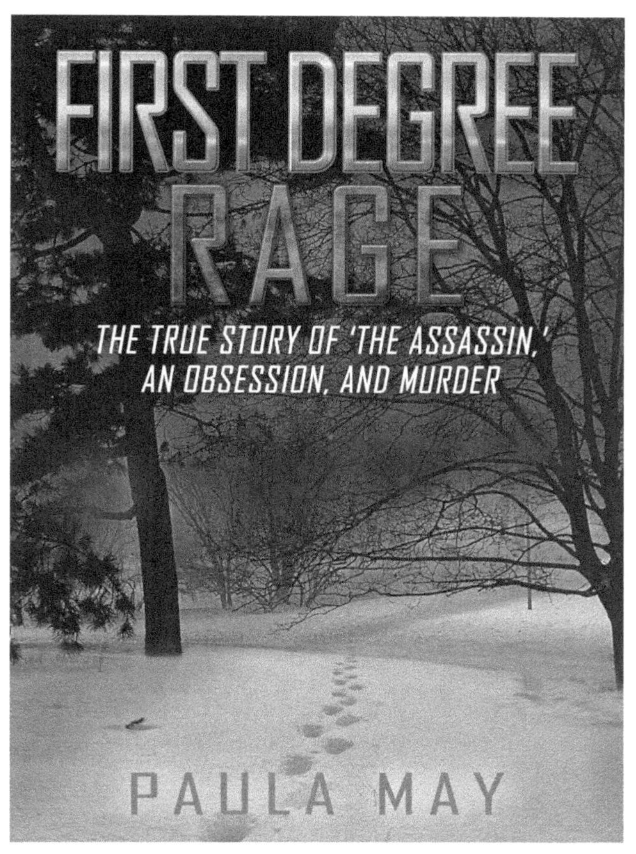

FIRST DEGREE RAGE BY PAULA MAY

https://wbp.bz/fdra

ALSO PUBLISHED BY WILDBLUE PRESS

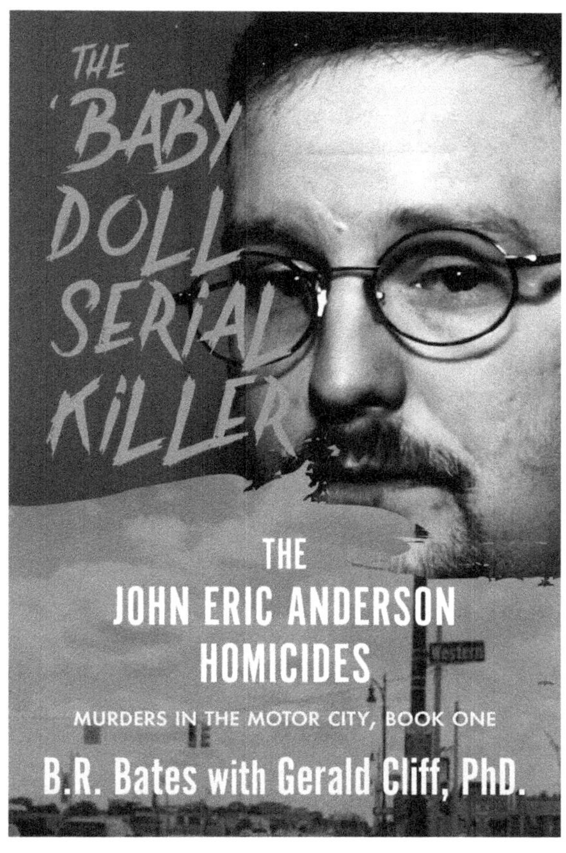

THE BABY DOLL SERIAL KILLER BY
B.R. BATES AND GERALD CLIFF

https://wbp.bz/babydoll

www.ingramcontent.com/pod-product-compliance
Lightning Source LLC
Chambersburg PA
CBHW051411050726
47595CB00010B/4012